PRAISE FOR *Off Izaak Walton Road:*
The Grace That Comes Through Loss

"Many of our ailments, both personal and planetary, arise from the delusion that humans are separate from the rest of nature. Laura Julier knows better. This lyrical memoir chronicles how she recovered from 'losses and wounds' by communing with the land, waters, and creatures in a patch of Iowa that has claimed her heart. While that cherished place suffers from climate disruption and sprawl, it still provides her with a nurturing home. Readers of this book, reminded of their membership in the web of life, may find their own sorrows eased."—Scott Russell Sanders, author of *The Way of Imagination*

"Not since Annie Dillard's *Pilgrim at Tinker Creek* have I been so consistently moved and roundly inspired by a woman's journey deeper into the natural world and deeper into her own human quest for understanding. Laura Julier is a brilliant inquirer, a humble investigator, and an eloquent guide to landscapes within and beyond the self. She asks hard questions: *Is this a place of neglect or refuge? What was it that made it so difficult to speak up and to name what I sought?* At one point, she names the hardest answer, what all love does: 'I am bringing into my life something that will break my heart.' If you're lifting this book off the shelf, turning to the first page, then you are also bringing something into your life that will break your heart—though not in vain. *Off Izaak Walton Road: The Grace That Comes Through Loss* is a book worth loving. At every turn, Julier reveals more beauty and wisdom in the rupture."—Julie Marie Wade, author of *Otherwise: Essays*

"In this moving memoir, Laura Julier seeks to 'return to the lessons of paying attention' within a beautiful yet fragile Midwestern place. In doing so, she discovers a world of natural wonders—the songs of winter owls and spring peepers, the colors of summer daylilies and wild roses, the signs of deep geologic time in the earth beneath her feet. Inwardly, as well, she explores her own heart's longing, in the face of loss, for healing and understanding. Wherever you live, this book will lead you toward a newly meaningful—and essential—relationship to home."—John T. Price, author of *All Is Leaf: Essays and Transformations*

"In this lyric memoir, Laura Julier takes us on a journey through long-held feelings of loss and grief—experienced through various landscapes—until she lands in a cabin along the Iowa River, a place neglected and damaged, yet abounding in wildlife. *Off Izaak Walton Road* shows the power of natural places to heal both themselves and those who carefully attend to them. Julier finds the hidden beauty and quiet life still thriving after derechos and historic floods. From barred owls fledging in a damaged silver maple to beavers damming a culvert, she notices the exquisite amongst the discarded and ties it to her own journey of self-discovery and emotional redemption."—Mary Swander, author of *The Maverick M.D.*

Off Izaak Walton Road

RIVER TEETH LITERARY NONFICTION PRIZE
Daniel Lehman and Joe Mackall, *Series Editors*

The River Teeth Literary Nonfiction Prize is awarded to the best work of literary nonfiction submitted to the annual contest sponsored by *River Teeth: A Journal of Nonfiction Narrative*.

Also available in the River Teeth Literary Nonfiction Prize series:

Aligning the Glacier's Ghost: Essays on Solitude and Landscape by
    Sarah Capdeville
Disequilibria: Meditations on Missingness by Robert Lunday
What Cannot Be Undone: True Stories of a Life in Medicine by
    Walter M. Robinson
The Rock Cycle: Essays by Kevin Honold
Try to Get Lost: Essays on Travel and Place by Joan Frank
I Am a Stranger Here Myself by Debra Gwartney
MINE: Essays by Sarah Viren
Rough Crossing: An Alaskan Fisherwoman's Memoir
    by Rosemary McGuire
The Girls in My Town: Essays by Angela Morales

OFF IZAAK WALTON ROAD

The Grace That Comes Through Loss

Laura Julier

University of New Mexico Press | Albuquerque

Library of Congress Cataloging-in-Publication Data
Names: Julier, Laura, 1952– author. Title: Off Izaak Walton Road: the grace that
comes through loss / Laura Julier. Other titles: River teeth literary nonfiction
prize (Series)
Description: Albuquerque: University of New Mexico Press, 2025. | Series:
River teeth literary nonfiction prize
Identifiers: LCCN 2024028338 (print) | LCCN 2024028339 (ebook) |
ISBN 9780826367716 (paperback) | ISBN 9780826367723 (epub)
Subjects: LCSH: Julier, Laura, 1952- | Women college teachers—United
States—Biography. | Women authors—Biography. | Place attachment. |
Johnson County (Iowa) | LCGFT: Autobiographies.
Classification: LCC LB2332.32.J85 2025 (print) | LCC LB2332.32 (ebook) |
DDC 378.1/2092—dc23/eng/20240702
LC record available at https://lccn.loc.gov/2024028338
LC ebook record available at https://lccn.loc.gov/2024028339

Founded in 1889, the University of New Mexico sits on the traditional homelands of the Pueblo of Sandia. The original peoples of New Mexico—Pueblo,
Navajo, and Apache—since time immemorial have deep connections to the land
and have made significant contributions to the broader community statewide.
We honor the land itself and those who remain stewards of this land throughout the generations and also acknowledge our committed relationship to
Indigenous peoples. We gratefully recognize our history.

Cover photograph courtesy of the author
Designed by Felicia Cedillos
Composed in Adobe Caslon Pro

For Kate

Contents

PART IV: EARTH ⋏ MARSH ⋏ SKIN

PART V: RIVER ⋏ NIGHT ⋏ PRAYER

PART VI: THE LOCKED CABIN, THE SWOLLEN RIVER, THE RIVEN ROAD, THE OPEN HEART

Preface
Holy place

I could tell you that when I was a child—three or four years old, not
more than that—I heard God in the snow. But that is not what happened. That would be a story overlaid in adulthood, which makes one
kind of sense of what happened. Making sense would come much
later, a response to others' need to understand. I had understood quite
well without words, without story. What I knew at the time was a hole
in the world, a whole world, a holy world.

We lived in a tiny suburban shoebox house with a postage stamp
yard. It was morning, I was whining loudly, and my mother with two
even younger children was overwhelmed. We were in the kitchen and
she was fed up, had reached her limit, had no more for me. She shoved
on my snowsuit, boots, hat, gloves, and pushed me out the back door.
It had snowed a lot the night before. Nothing had been cleared. The
door, as she opened it, swept aside what had fallen or was leaning into
it. She slammed shut the inside door, relieved to be relieved of me, I'm
sure. I suspect she was trying to teach me a lesson.

What happened was this. I stopped crying immediately. My eyes
widened. I heard nothing—a nothing that was something. A huge
silence. That's all there was. The world had shrunk, the world had
grown enormous. All I could see from where I had been plunked
down was the steps, the stoop, the short stretch from there to the large
red beech in the middle of the yard, back by the silver stockade fence,
the garage to the left, the tips of the hedge line of deep-red sticker
bushes on the right, the roof overhang above me, the cedar reaching

toward it. That's all there was, and it was everything. The world had come through a hole, into the space I could see, sitting on the snow piled on the concrete step outside the back door. It was loud silence, silence that spoke, spoke to me and with me, sweeping me into all creation.

I knew I was in the presence of something huge, something transcendent, something of awe. And I knew it was home. I recognized it, had known it before, belonged there, knew it to be unchanging. I did not try to move, nor want to.

I remember nothing else. I don't know how long I stayed there, or what my mother said when she opened the door again, but I have a sense of having come inside quieted, residing deep within myself.

At one point, I believed that in this place on a gravel road along the Iowa River, I had found it again. I believed that in this place I was in the presence of the holy, and that in this place I would find my own wholeness, my own holiness.

▲

The loss and sorrow that I refer to in the pages that follow have their origins in many points in time and in events that took place both before and after that morning on the back step. In these pages, I have sought to create a record of the psychic landscape that those experiences and events left with and in me, a record of memory more powerful than any literal or objective recounting of their details. I have tried to write the emotional ecology that I carried with me into my adult life and that eventually brought me to a cabin alongside a river, off Izaak Walton Road.

Overture
Early March, off Izaak Walton Road

If you can get out the door early, quickly enough, and head down the road away from the river toward open fields, toward the quarry, you can see the end of dawn, an orange crowning, bleeding on the horizon. You can look squarely at the forbidden.

You can turn and see a ribbon of pink slice the trees; if you are still, you can see them shiver, grateful.

You can see a red-tailed hawk flash from the trees on the road ahead of you, then another, like guilty lovers, caught, anxious not to be noticed.

By then, day has flooded everywhere; you can turn back. And maybe as you reach the river, the cabin door, and the fire inside, the bald eagle will have stirred, dropping out of a high oak, coasting eye level in front of you, then circling upriver.

Listen.

It is early March. Sun breaks horizon over the pony shed in the back pasture at six twenty-five. Hurry. Leave now. You do not know who lingers, who's waiting, what will be swooping low over the river one last time before moving north, where ice is breaking up. You do not know what waits around the bend or what your watchfulness will bring to light.

PART I

SNOW ⋏ FIRE ⋏ SILENCE

Fire rearranges light the way light reorders landscape.

—GRETEL EHRLICH, "LANDSCAPE"

Often I am permitted to return to a meadow
as if it were a scene made-up by the mind,
that is not mine, but is a made place,

that is mine, it is so near to the heart,
an eternal pasture folded in all thought

—ROBERT DUNCAN,
"OFTEN I AM PERMITTED TO RETURN TO A MEADOW"

Once I owned a house

ONCE I OWNED A house. It was a small house in Iowa City, near Plum Grove, the home of Iowa's first governor. It had begun as a corner grocery store in the early 1900s, but its overlarge back door was the only part that still looked like what it had been. Its interior walls were flimsy and its four rooms tiny. In the deep backyard was an old plum tree, an enormous pussy willow tree, a thicket of raspberry canes, lilac bushes, and a large black walnut tree back where it bordered the alley.

Although I owned it for only eight years and those eight years are long ago, even now if I am quiet, I can hear its sounds—a dog barking behind the alley, a child's voice, a father calling, the padded hush of thick gardens, the boards on the back deck and the brush of snow on the windows. These are the sounds embedded in my blood and my bones. When I close my eyes, I can hear them no matter where I am. I do not have to tap my heels three times. I know the smell of earth under the raspberries, the shade of the buds on the lilac bush in the far back corner where I buried the divorce papers, can remember in my bones the rhythmic thuds when someone walks up the five steps to the front door. For years afterward, my arm muscles and nerve pathways and internal clocks were all still finely attuned to that house, its sounds, its angles.

Although I owned it for only eight years, they may as well have been twenty-eight. In that house I lived with my first cat, Penelope. I learned to till a garden, to turn in compost, learned that blood meal will repel rabbits, that tomatoes can't grow too close to black walnut trees. I learned to transplant things—it began with chrysanthemums and irises—to find and kill squash bugs by hand, to save seeds and start them early. That garter snakes hang in raspberry canes and that fledgling cardinals leave their nests before they can fly. I learned to can vegetables and to make jam from the fruit of the mulberry tree by the front curb.

In this house, I carved pumpkins, carefully inserted candles, then lined them on the front porch. I put up a Christmas tree and hosted potlucks. I gave shelter to friends and made room for visiting family. I'd filled this house with the steam of jasmine tea in winter and peonies from May's garden. In July, I would rise early and pick raspberries in the yard, black on the left, red on the right. It wasn't until I lived in this house, well into my thirties, that I began to feel, to find, and to shape a home. To plant a garden and bring its fruits to my neighbors.

While I lived in this house, I walked the neighborhood streets every day as a way to know the place. The back screen door would slam as I left the house early in the morning, at sunrise, heading to the alley, up the slight rise of Ginter Avenue, turning on Yewell at Jody's house, past Wild Bill's, over to Highland and past the rectory, turning left on Lower Muscatine past the stone cottages and Moffitt houses, then home to eat breakfast on the back steps. On summer nights when the heat and humidity made sleeping unbearable, I walked the streets barefoot at midnight. At midnight in winter, I'd shovel the two long legs of sidewalk that met at the corner, then lie down in the snow and let silence take over.

At first, I believed my life in this house would be temporary and brief. I spent hours on the phone, sitting on the orange shag carpet, struggling with a cord stretched too taut by a separation I had believed would be easy to handle. In this house, I'd been married, and in this house, I found myself alone again. In the face of that rupture, I clung to the house and the yard, and the garden and the years' turning, and in them I found a bit of safe and solid ground. Feet rooted, I found room to look around, to breathe unhindered, to begin to understand some of the violence of my early life.

In this house, I began to grow roots, to know time passing in one place. Mourned the pussy willow when it blew over in a storm. Saw the gallon-sized arborvitae that I'd planted grow to reach over my head, watched the children across the street emerge from diapers to kindergarten to two-wheelers. So much that has remained true and deep and knit into my bones I found while living in this house.

In the back of my mind—on its shadowy scrim, where images and people flit behind our eyes and whisper when we are not thinking—I had seen myself grow old in this house. Outside my bedroom window, I watched Ola two doors over in her housedress stand in the morning sun, extending her arms to their length with unexpected vigor, running her fingers through waist-length gray hair to dry it. I would smile, smear peanut butter for the birds on the plum tree out back, no longer caring how foolish I looked, tutored years before by another old woman for whom I had cared and who had taught me much. I wanted to be these old women, in this house, and have the years of growth and change so seep into my bones that even clouded eyes and dimmed hearing would not keep me from knowing its sounds, its seasons.

▲

That house and neighborhood and eastern Iowa landscape of rolling hills resembled nowhere I had lived as a child or young adult. There was nothing that resonated. Yet somehow as soon as I'd sat down on the banks of the Iowa River, I knew myself to be home. It's where I found enough space to wrestle myself free of the strictures of circumstances and inheritance. Physical landscape and spiritual geography mapped over each other, intertwined like the vines creeping along the alleyways in back, along the neglected paths and secret places.

A hollow yearning with no name, no object, had lingered and persisted; its haunting soundtrack had followed me for decades, from my earliest memories, unvoiced but palpable. It wasn't the streets of New York City, nor its suburbs. Nor the farms down the road as I was beginning school. Nor the affluent, all-white, upwardly mobile community of increasingly expansive and expensive homes carved out of the woodlands along Long Island's North Shore. Nor the side streets I wandered as an adolescent in city neighborhoods called Little Something, early attempts to find a place I recognized. As housing developments ate up potato farms and blueberry woods, and new kids arrived at school, we asked one another, "What are you?"—meaning "Where are your parents or grandparents from?" I wanted to find the place I came from and belonged, a homeland, but it was not anywhere I looked. I wanted stories and a language to explain the losses I felt tearing at my throat yet could not name. The three grandparents alive long enough for me to know them each carried vestiges of a former homeland on their tongues, in their foods, in their memories. But none of them spoke about a place.

I think of how long and how much I resented that my mother would not talk about the land her parents left to come to the tenements of New York. Would not even entertain the idea of making a trip to find out. Would not acknowledge until I was an adult that she knew the language, remembered its cadences and vocabulary from childhood. How much I wanted her to teach me something other than how to cover loss with shame and silence.

What was it that made it so difficult to speak up and to name what I sought? Everything, and nothing. Everything having to do with being a grandchild of immigrants, a child of the transition from one social stratum to another, a quiet child, a small child, a girl child, a first child—the one they learned on, my mother said, the model, the hope, the disappointment. And nothing at all worth saying, given the more visible and deadly oppressions of racism and poverty and genocide all around me. The rules about how to be a girl. "Don't pay attention to that praise, you'll get a big head." How to be a child in my father's house. "Don't raise your voice or I'll smack you across the face. Don't speak unless you're spoken to." How to be a child of a child of immigrants. "Why do you want to know about them? They're all dead, they're from the old country, they're ignorant—they're not us." Of living with too many people in too little space, and several varieties of forced intimacies.

Everything, and nothing. Nothing in the details themselves. Yet all those details came together into an emotional landscape I ran from. Ran first to the end of the block, where I created hidden houses in the woods with castoffs from construction sites, as housing tracts erased the woods. Ran away from home twice before I was thirteen, on a bus headed for any other state. Ran from the suburbs into the city, then to the farthest college I could earn a scholarship to. I ran away to marriage, to a man who was himself an immigrant, and the first chance I got, migrated to the other edge of the continent.

"You're from New York," I was repeatedly told every time I opened my mouth, as if I didn't know. As if I needed reminding—which I must have, because by then, I was trying to change my voice. By then, I had learned what the view was like from anywhere west of the Hudson River, those far distances on the well-known cover of the *New Yorker* magazine. What everyone else thinks of New Yorkers: arrogant, competitive, cutthroat, abrasive, parochial, myopic. There were plenty of stories about where I was from, but none of them were mine.

The abuses and fragmentation that shaped my preadult life all felt personal, singular, individual. Disabling. Silent and silencing. I did not yet understand the ways they might be political and systemic. In response, I walked the edge and took risks. Not the stuff that made risk heroic. I put myself into places I shouldn't have, chose badly lit city streets, alone, at night. I actively pursued edges, testing and pushing myself, unwaveringly certain I would not fall.

And then, a few years later, I stopped running. By then, I'd moved five more times, to five different states, and I was tired. By the time I came to the house in Iowa City, I had grown tired of having to act as if I knew what I was doing, tired of what it cost to forget how easily I could stumble. Tired of being Marge Piercy's strong woman, "standing on tiptoe and lifting a barbell while trying to sing Boris Godunov." Tired of the anxiety I choked down for every meal, of naming it only to feel hands at my back pushing me out front again. I was looking for a safe place, and in this town in the shoebox house on this corner lot, I found one for a time. At first, every night before I got into bed, I'd lock all the doors and windows and then, to be even more certain, I'd slide the bolt on my side of the basement door. I found myself walking home one brilliantly sunny day at noon, along a sidewalk arched over railroad tracks, speaking out loud to no one, "I'm terrified . . . terrified," over and over, my mouth tasting each separate syllable of a word and a conjugation I'd never said, never known, never considered before.

▲

And then I had to leave. With a job offer in a different city, I was forced to sell. On the morning that I left the house for good, Ola appeared next door with her long gray hair freshly wet, standing in her garden like an apparition. This morning, she did not look up and wave. I went back into the house one last time. "Have your feelings," my father had said on the phone the night before, "but when you leave, close the door and don't look back." Which is of course what his parents had done, what my mother insisted her parents do. I had dug up a few more perennials, unscrewed some fixtures from the walls, and met the man who was buying the house. He was quiet, and he, too, had an old cat he worried about. I told him where the tulip bulbs were planted and how to care for the furnace. I spent the day lost in a litany: this is the last time I'll ever hear the cats' feet on the basement steps, this is the last morning I'll ever wake to the garbage collector's truck, this is the last time I'll hear the back door slam and echo off the garage across the alley.

On the deck of the SS *Aquitania*, sailing from her home in August of 1923, did the thirty-four-year-old Katarzyna feel that anguish of loss? Would she have allowed it? In a series of photographs, which I used to believe was all I had from this grandmother, she leans from the window of one or another of all the apartments she lived in for the rest of her life, framed always by lush and persistent roses. For me, they stand as a sign of the home she never saw again. Is that why I dig up and carry with me clumps of fibrous peony tubers and root balls of yellow chrysanthemums from one place to another, leaving some behind, foisting them on friends and neighbors, spreading—or securing—pieces of a home lost long before I was born?

I passed on the stories, handed over the keys. But I couldn't follow my father's advice. What filled the back seat of my car as I drove away was not the plants or the cats but the weight of loss. It sat leaden above the wheel wells, it trailed off in doubt. It ran like the soundtrack at the end of a movie, as the camera pulls back and music tears at your breathing. Loss followed me to the next place, and the next.

In conversations with friends and family members spread across the continent, I tried to explain why leaving that house was a loss like death. Why despite a good job in a different midwestern city, I was not happy. Why I inwardly yearned for and outwardly rhapsodized about a quite ordinary place. I never found the words. How do you explain attachment to a place? When I lost my marriage, friends were kind, sympathetic, patient. They gave me time to grieve. When I lost my house, there was a moment of sympathy but no one was patient. It was time to move on, they said. I gave up on words and on trying to explain. Much of the time, I fell into an old habit, believing that what I know to be true is instead a sign of misalignment, emotional disturbance, or some deeper miscue. I practiced denial and silenced myself. I dwelt in amnesia.

For years afterward, the smallest thing could pull me back to that house: to the matted web of light, the early-spring musk of molded leaves, the ethereal geography of longing mapped onto each bloom and bud in its yard. For years, I tamped down these memories, stayed far away and eluded their draw. I managed to breathe evenly and recite only the story of surfaces: I had owned a house, I had sold it, I had left town.

All I knew in those days was that it was yet another loss.

This is not the place

AFTER SEVEN YEARS TEACHING and publishing and doing all the requisite other work at a major university in a town in which I tried but failed to feel at home, I was granted tenure. With tenure, I could no longer maintain the fiction to myself that I was living in Michigan only temporarily. I had to buy a house.

The file of printouts of each property I went to see, each Sunday's open house, each trip I made with a real estate agent, contains over 150 separate documents. For a year and a half, I looked, trying to find a certain feel and siting, a landscape that hearkened back to that house I had owned in Iowa City. I asked only for a fireplace and a flat, spacious yard in which to plant a large vegetable garden. I needed the back door to open directly out onto the land—no side doors onto the driveway, no raised ranches or split-levels. I needed to have the kitchen facing east and the living room facing west, and so the first thing I did when I walked into each house was orient myself, looking not at the walls or floors or appliances but out the windows, to get my bearings. I rejected many of those houses without a complete tour because I couldn't get the ground under my feet fast enough or directly enough from inside. Any wall facing the backyard was an obstruction, an enclosure that kept me from breathing. It was not just a set of walls I was buying but an inside space connected to an outside space.

After a year and a half of open houses and scheduled viewings, I bought a house built into the side of a hill—the only hill in Lansing, a capital city intentionally sited in the mid-1800s on drained swamp.

On this property, there is not a single square foot of flat ground, and no fireplace. I can't tell you why I bought it. I rejected it outright as soon as we drove up, my realtor appearing more and more deaf to my preferences, though to his credit, outwardly and unfailingly patient. He no doubt understood far more quickly than I did that I was looking for a landscape that did not exist anywhere in Lansing, Michigan, but only in memory and longing.

I bought the house in May and immediately left town.

I spent the months of the following summer looking for a place to spend my sabbatical, a rest or retreat from all the striving. I found myself in one after another of five different places, jerked from one site to another, exploring and arranging the space, settling in and then, having wrapped myself in comfort, forced to move again.

I fled to Prince Edward Island in the North Atlantic. Sat day after day in an Adirondack chair overlooking the Northumberland Strait while hours passed but not a single car on the road below. I found two houses I tried to rent for the coming winter. Then, for reasons unclear to me still, I was following the rocky, marshy Atlantic shore of northern Maine to a tiny town where a colleague owned a house she had offered for rent. But when I called her, she'd changed her mind. I drove on and tucked myself in among the White Mountains, the pine and spruce forest floors redolent in the sun, the lake waters deep and still chilled. I returned to the hills along the Hudson River valley in upstate New York that I'd known as a child. Valleys that once had small towns and farm stands, dairy stores, and place-names in Dutch or some transformation of an Indian word, but now showed signs of gentrification. I stared at real estate ads and rental notices.

It was as if someone kept yanking me out of the ground, turning me over, examining the roots. What *is* this thing? How will it grow? What does it need?

I made my way to a small village in western Ukraine, the home my grandparents had left seventy-five years before and was at that time eastern Poland, reaching for a grounding that was not and could not be mine. I was trying to understand things it had never occurred to me to ask. Why my mother had never spoken or asked about her parents' home until after they were dead. Why my preadolescent self had twice run away from home. Why I had loved that one house I'd owned as if it were an extension of my body, felt its loss like an amputation. Why I had not been able to imagine or make myself choose a different option than leaving Iowa City to begin with, when I did not want to. Why in all my telling the sentences place me in the object position, subject to any force but my own choice.

And why I had finally bought this other house, but was so unhappy that I didn't live in it for the first six months I owned it.

In the end, I found that these were not the right questions at all, but it took me several years to come to know that. What matters at this point in the telling is that I was repeating a pattern I did not yet recognize.

It began like this

I FIRST ENCOUNTERED R in the pages of a book. My mentor and friend Carl had just published it, a book about weather and gardening, about food and Kate, his wife, about coming to the end of his teaching career, and about the life he and Kate had crafted over thirty years in a century-old house on a hill in the Goosetown neighborhood of Iowa City. R appears in the book briefly, fleetingly, helping Kate with the sixty-foot perennial beds at the back and top of the sweeping lawn behind their house.

She appeared in the flesh one day in late September of my sabbatical, her truck crunching up the gravel drive at Carl and Kate's. I had been expecting her for a month. I was sitting up in the third-floor garret of their house, where each morning for thirty days, under steep, angled ceilings lined with deeply oiled wood bookcases and reading nooks tucked into each gable, I had been trying to write.

In this place, ten years before, I had listened to Carl comment as my advisor on the writing project that would allow me to finish a graduate degree and force me to leave my home in Iowa City for a job elsewhere. His responses were rigorous and passionate, offered with unfailing care and support and an assumption that we shared the same fierce commitment to precise, graceful language. In that room, Carl had coaxed final revisions. "Look. Begin like this," he'd say, and almost start writing the sentences for me. It had been a long haul.

In this place, years later, at a small wooden table facing a floor-to-peak window with a view out onto a sunken patio, the Doric columns of Kate's gazebo, his huge vegetable garden, an old pear tree, the wide lawn sloping up to swathes of perennial color and finally a wall of enormous spruce, Carl had retreated each evening for a year to write five hundred words, and in that way gradually accrued the pages of what came to be two books.

In this place now, I had been writing for a month. When I could not find any place to land for my sabbatical, I had come back to Iowa City and was living in this house as temporary caretaker while Kate and Carl traveled west. The opportunity had been pure serendipity; I couldn't believe my luck. I sat at the keyboard each morning and wrote my own daily pages, an account of what was growing, what I harvested, changes in weather and foliage, evidence of creatures and changes. Each afternoon, I walked downtown, winding through quiet, lush side streets and alleys. I was content in a way I had not been in the decade since I'd left Iowa City. I didn't bother to try to explain this to anyone, except as the end of September drew nearer and I faced having to return to Michigan and a house I hated.

Carl had given me explicit and detailed instructions for what to pay attention to, what to pick and when, how to cook it, how to freeze it, how to protect it from deer. But I had been told not to worry about the perennial beds because R would come to take care of them. The heavy heat of late-August days and nights had given way to cooler nights, cooler rains, late September's harvest moon hanging full over the hill, blurred by light fog as the heated earth met evening air. I felt the weight of precedence; I felt the weight of obligation. I looked out the window one morning and there was R, walking up the dew-soaked lawn, sunlight still just above the horizon, drenching everything with a lemon wash.

We sat on the stone ledge of the gazebo choking mugs of tea, our elbows tight, shoulders hunched against the chill. "Man, I can't stand it. I'm so cold my nipples hurt." Her voice was husky, like a smoker's. Murray, her butterscotch-and-white shaggy dog, was patient. It wasn't really cold but cold was coming, and for the past few years, R had been leaving town as soon as it did, heading south to a small village on the shore of Belize. We exchanged bits of information, talked as strangers do. Carl and Kate, absent, were a thin connecting thread we each held tentatively, skirting privacy. For half an hour we sat, then I went back up to the garret desk and she dragged an oilcloth tarp up the hill and began to clean and weed and deadhead. Wiry, deeply tanned, with long, stringy blond hair hanging loose, she worked harder and faster than anyone I'd ever seen. From the third floor, I watched the canvas of Kate's garden emerge newly textured, with brush strokes of color and lines more clearly defined. In a couple of hours, she dragged the loaded tarp back down the hill and was gone. The next day and the next, we sat and talked on the cold stone ledge till we warmed, and then each went back to work.

When Carl and Kate returned, R and I spent an afternoon sipping pinot grigio on the sandstone patio with them, listening to tales of their trek through the Canadian Rockies. A few days later, before I left to drive back to Michigan, I followed directions to R's place south of town, off a dirt road, next to the river. We had agreed that I would come back in a month to live in her cabin for the remainder of my sabbatical, take care of Murray the dog and Inky the cat while she escaped from the coming cold of November and December. She told me where the keys were hidden, warned me about the landowner, who plowed the road, periodically clear-cut the woods, and whose bills for access kept rising. She showed me how to keep the woodstove going and how to call the cat. "It's so hard for me to leave them, you know? I couldn't leave them unless I knew someone would take care of them, that you would care for them like your own," she said.

"What will you do with your cats?" she asked, suddenly anxious. "What will happen with them when you come here?" A complicated but convenient choreography was unfolding. A student of mine needed to get away from family and was happy to have the chance to live on her own with my cats. My need to be in Iowa City, R's need to be barefoot in Belize—we shared a certain kind of tug on the heart that deep desire for a place brings.

What was said in those few handfuls of minutes to foster this kind of trust? What tests did we each pass with the other that got us to this point? How was it we tumbled into the landscape of each other's lives so completely in those very few days? Nothing about where this part of the story leads or has ended makes as much sense as the meager threads of its beginning.

Izaak Walton Road

FROM TOWN, YOU HEAD south on Riverside Drive, which runs, true to its name, along the west side of the river. At the end of a workday when you're heading south, you are driving between sharp bluffs rising on your right, behind which the sun is setting, and on your left, the river. And across that, a hill called the Pentacrest, where the first capital of the territory of Iowa was sited and on which sits gold-domed Old Capitol, gathering the light of sunset.

At what used to be the southern edge of town, Riverside Drive becomes Old Highway 218, and as you keep heading south, the scenery turns gritty. Sturgis Ferry Park—site of the first ferry crossing for residents of the town to get from one side to the other—is nothing more than a garbage can, a covered picnic table, and a dirt turn-in that becomes a boat ramp. In winter when the sun melts snow, Canada geese seem to find something worth pecking around at, but you couldn't really call it grass in summer. Farther south are a few grain elevators, the university printing office, Moore Business Forms, Hubbard Feeds, and a fenced auto salvage yard.

You pass the Army Reserve headquarters, jeeps lined up behind chain link fencing, and the weed-filled parking lot of the Colonial Lanes bowling alley. You also pass the Iowa City Municipal Airport. Driving south near dinner hour, or north along Riverside in the mornings, I have seen tiny propeller planes coming in to land, low to the road in front of me, low to the chain link fencing at the start of the runway.

Few people in Iowa City pay attention to this, the oldest general aviation airport west of the Mississippi, because for years now all commercial air traffic has been centered twenty-three miles north, in Cedar Rapids. The Iowa City Municipal Airport's three 4,100-foot runways are concrete, five to six feet deep in some places, made to handle the heavy use they got as a primary flight training base for World War II pilots. Each is angled differently, "which is great for flight training," I was told by Clay Johnson, an employee of Jet Air who answered the phone one breezy Saturday morning, "because if you're not too good at landing into the wind, you want to be able to go a different direction when the wind is bad."

When you've passed the airport and the grain elevators and the trailer park, you get to the Iowa City Ready Mix, and beyond that, Croell Redi-Mix, and if there's any wind at all, you have to roll up your windows as clouds of concrete dust whip left to right across the road. On the right are the Johnson County 4-H Fairgrounds, and beyond that a large wooded hill—Ryerson's Woods—skirted by a wide grass field. You can park and hike trails up and over that hill.

Just at the point where you've got the dust from Croell's on your left and Ryerson's Woods rising on your right, the road veers around the hill, to the right and away from the river.

You turn left onto Oak Crest Hill Road and the river, too, turns left, away from a southern flow, turning on itself, first east and north, then south again in a classic oxbow. But you can't see this from the road.

Oak Crest Hill Road is the continuation of old 218, a two-lane road running between the new US 218 on its right and railroad tracks on its left. The new 218 was, at one point, part of an intricate network of highways that made up the Avenue of the Saints, planned to make an easy flow from St. Louis to St. Paul. The train tracks are almost never in use, though for a stretch of about four days once, a long line of ADM tanker cars mysteriously appeared, disappeared, appeared, disappeared, day after day, always parked, never in motion.

A quarter mile down Oak Crest Hill Road, you turn left again onto

Izaak Walton Road. You turn left, that is, if you can see it, and in the dark the only way you can see it is if your headlights illuminate the crooked road sign or the railroad crossing sign. In the daylight, you might notice a weatherworn green-and-yellow-painted plywood sign pointing to "Johnson County Chapter—Izaak Walton League."

You turn left and bump over a collection of permanent potholes, then over the railroad tracks, and down a paved road past a stand of trees, a field of corn, a marsh, a gravel pit, the Johnson County Quarry, and the Izaak Walton League.

Most people I ask aren't aware of anything worth noting south of the Johnson County 4-H Fairgrounds except the Izaak Walton League. People might go to the fairgrounds for the Mennonite relief sale in late May or for a community theater production. Some people still take Oak Crest Hill Road rather than the interstate to go ten miles south to the small town of Hills. But unless you are a dump truck driver or one of the ten or twelve people who live there, you have no reason to go down Izaak Walton Road, and once down the road, little way of knowing that there is anything beyond the entrance to S&G Materials Company, where the paved road ends. The Izaak Walton League—sited between the Johnson County Quarry, Johnson County Auto Recycling, and the marsh, across from the S&G gravel pit—is the only parcel along Izaak Walton Road where the grass is mowed regularly, the only place that doesn't look like it's been abandoned to industrial uses. A very long gravel drive lined with tall weigela and smaller forsythia leads back to a large wooden hall, picnic tables and fire pits, a roughhewn clubhouse and wide lawns.

Izaak Walton Road ends when the concrete ends—when the road splits like the tines of a dinner fork running parallel, all dirt and gravel, for about another quarter mile. It's the left-hand tine, Camino del Rio, that you follow to get to R's place.

You bump from concrete to gravel, pass a couple of houses between the road and the river, then enter a tunnel of trees wide enough for one car only. The road curves sharply left, skirting a fenced pasture, and heads straight for the river, at the last minute curving sharply right.

Then road and river run parallel, a bit of grass and trees between them. As you make that last curve, you might catch glimpses on the right of a blue one-story dwelling nestled deeply among gardens and groves, its space shaped and sculpted by low rock walls. A secret garden place, carefully tended, unlike any of the other parcels.

From Izaak Walton Road, you would never know this was here. From here, you would not know about the gravel pits, the quarry, the rumbling of the dump trucks, the potholes or railroad tracks. From behind the stands of sixty-to-eighty-foot walnut, oak, and sycamore, and the thick wall of juniper, hemlock, and white pine surrounding R's place as I drove up that day at the end of September, you could feel quite removed, hidden, nested, safe.

Loss

VOICES OF MONASTIC CHANT. One solid silver note, rising, falling, effortlessly. Polyphonic lines diverging, then moving together, so perfectly an untrained ear thinks they are the same note. Droning, reciting, modes of moving across the intervals, one moment, one semitone to the next. *Parallelismus membrorum*, two halves of prayer. Each note sent from silence returns to silence, like breath, like fire, raised, sent forth, surrendered. Departing, then returning. A sustaining call over the moving waters. Points of silence, rest. *Non finalis.*

Voices high like an oboe's thin, reeded call: the call of the geese on the river, huddled—or above, approaching, landing. Gliding in and out of synchrony. Unaccompanied, calling, echoing, alone.

Snow falling. Falling. Falling. A filmed sequence, silent, the lens unmoving, the land and brush and riverbank accumulating. Absorbing all sound. Any sound is singular, bounds distances, skipping downriver on snow mounded on dried grasses, hollowed refuges, soft sculpted, absorbing, covering. Snow descending all afternoon, through dusk and night. At night the land is white, the sky is white, the turns in the road, the paths where deer enter to lie down, are all white. Only the river is dark, a ribbon of velvet carrying the weight of scales downstream, out of sight.

I walk the road. The dog loves the snow. The trees are not yet topped by sunrising pink and yellow. From a tree branch I pass but have not yet seen, an eagle drops away from us, gliding downriver. There is no sound. Two rusted metal chairs angled toward each other, a mound of fire ash between, gauze draped, silenced.

Late fall. I've come to the cabin on the edge of the Iowa River, in the darkening days of fall's dying. I have come to ponder loss. I live the echoes, the deeper notes of a different harmonic line, the notes my own voice recognizes, takes solace in, can match. I have come to try to take care of the sorrow at my core, the well of longing I carry and have carried for so long, to figure out if I will ever be comforted, or ever always only longing.

The dog walks the gravel road, the snow rutted in one pair of parallel lines. We walk into that sound, those two halves of prayer, notes high enough that throat strains, eyebrows raise, not to reach the note but with longing, with loss, with tears that fall, fall, fall. Or do not, because there is the snow, the notes, the eagle flying downriver, away, away, the fire at home, the woods at dusk, the river flowing velvet and silent, the geese huddled, calling.

Days' waning light

I sit in the front room of a cabin lined with windows almost to the floor on two walls, a fireplace on the third. The windows bring the outside in—the trees, the bend in the river, the dusk, the geese, the snow-heavy sky. I've managed to figure out how to keep the cast-iron stove going all night and have settled into an easy routine.

Every morning, I awake to a butterscotch dog and a black cat curled with me on the bed. I get up and throw on gray sweat pants with mended holes all down the legs, a white stretched-out turtleneck, blue plaid flannel shirt, wool ragg socks, and R's felt clogs. I go outdoors, get wood to stoke the fires in the woodstove and fireplace. I brew coffee, open the back door for Murray the dog and Inky the cat, wait for their sounds, let them back in. I eat and write, stare out the windows or try to photograph the birds at the feeders, the ground, the tree stumps. I tune to the classical music station, listen for the weather at intervals, plan a short trip into town for groceries or down one of the country roads toward Kalona in the afternoon, and look forward to each day's ebbing of late fall and early winter's light.

DECEMBER 4

I have settled in to R's cabin as if I have been pulled in by the open arms of the spirit of the place. Immediately and deeply, as if I'd always known it. Nestled in pillows on the wicker couch, I look around and it's as if I have always lived here. As if every item on the walls, on the mantelpiece, on the shelves, every piece of pottery or glass, every jar of shells has been placed there by me. As if I know all the stories, as if I had been the one to select and settle each thing into its right spot, groups and pieces arranged contrapuntally, maracas and drums and finger harps next to weather vanes and oil lamps. Posters of tropical flora and fauna next to decades-old farm calendars and prairie scenes, Depression-era vases beside reed baskets and lead crystal sherry glasses filled with tiny pink shells from Caribbean beaches.

R cries about leaving Murray and Inky whenever she calls from Belize. She tells me she would go more often and stay there longer if she could feel reassured about them back in Iowa. She tells me I am welcome to come live here whenever I want.

DECEMBER 6

Not half an hour after the soft voice on the radio tells of a storm to come and sub-zero wind chills tonight, snow starts to drift down, small tiny bits of it, barely noticeable and probably treacherous. The fire centers our attention; the animals sleep curled up, facing it. I face it too. In this place, weather shapes the day, shapes the particulars of living. I go out back for more wood before the snow gets too bad, shovel ashes out of the other stove, then run a hot bath and eat a sandwich. I start a pot of soup for dinner later, as the wind starts howling. I need to put up more plastic sheeting on the bedroom window, get to town to buy a live trap for the mice, which will probably be coming in again tonight, drawn to the warmth.

The day is shaped as I am led, by weather, by animals, by fire, by meals, by thought and wonder and a particular slant of light. Cardinal on the tree trunk, red against the grays and browns of winter woods, about six feet off the snow-crusted ground. Soft curves of a deep-green glass vase on the windowsill against the snow-heavy sky. There is so much to attend to, so much that old habits, fears, vigilance have taught me to ignore.

Every morning, a woodpecker lands on the tree stump to feed and I look up. By the time I reach for my camera and set the exposure, it is gone. We repeat this every day.

I've lit the woodstove off the bedroom because the temperature has gone way down and the wind has picked up. Last night's wind chills were below zero. I was awakened at 3:30 a.m. by Inky batting at the mousetrap, and when I walked outside in a corduroy shirt and wool slippers to release the thing down by the river, it didn't feel that cold. But she woke me again at 5:30, chasing another one into the bedroom behind my suitcase, and after I determined it had slipped through a crack under the door into the unheated back room, I found the fire had burned almost entirely down. And then at 7:30, when I realized the small and noisy backup furnace was kicking on every twenty minutes, I finally got up to start building up the fire, hauling in more wood, my attention drawn up by the high clouds, the icy clarity of the air, the V of geese circling over the river.

After the fires are going, Murray fed, Inky curled up in the still-warm nest of bedcovers my body has left, another mouse released, this time in the back garden, coffee made and the computer turned on, I sit down to work. I've been trying to explain, to myself and to others, the deep sense of well-being that wraps my shoulders with comfort and safety day after day here at this cabin on the Iowa River.

In this place there are a dozen bird feeders that are perpetually busy and needing to be filled. A fire that needs tending. And when I go outside, geese flying overhead call my attention upward. Every time I look up from writing or reading, what I see changes with the light. Pulled outside myself in these ways, I am rooted and grounded. I breathe more deeply, uncurl, unfurl into my own skin, into the space around me, a freedom I have not known before. Enough space to listen, to set my own rhythm.

And the quality of my attention is different here. I give my attention to the way the squirrel comes bounding over the limestone wall to bury the nut in its mouth in the small herb bed. The way the knobby branches of the forsythia bush, tucked up against the wood-pile, are matted and woven into a safe shelter. The way the cat follows the sun as it fills one window and then another. The way bits and pieces of this place are becoming part of a rhythm—like some umbilical exchange, or like noticing the joining of my heartbeat and my footstep—beginning to knit me to this place.

Solitude prepares the ground, and in solitude, I find solace and safety.

DECEMBER 13

The light slides out from behind slow-gathering clouds, brushed by the branches, flickering on the wall. I find comfort in the waning light of these days that approach the winter solstice. Days that find my spirit expanding, if spirit is what we call this swelling at the center, the thing that makes me widen my eyes and deepen my breath and know deeply that I am safe.

DECEMBER 14

Day after day spent in solitude. The shelter of this place is a gift, a landscape I have needed without knowing it. It calls up out of old, old memory the longing for a place like this, although nothing in memory—or in life—ever was like it. Only a few steps take me to a cup of tea, to the window ledge, out the door to the dirt road and river's edge. Everything, it seems, is cocooned, everything is within reach.

DECEMBER 15

Day after day touches some deep sorrow, some wound I cannot name. There is longing, there is sadness, even as there is, I realize, an emotion I have never known. I walk with Murray to the mailboxes, then beyond. Say the word: *joy*. So simple it becomes pure sound. A complicated sound, no history, no meaning. I can name the signs—expansive breathing, a lightness in the chest by which I know what is meant by my heart—but I'm like a child with no other words. All I can think is that I do not want to think about why I have never, in all the decades of memory, known it. Nor do I want to examine too much what has occasioned it. I walk down the road. I walk back into the woods, pushing aside the dried and withered abundance of summer, following matted trails. I stand in the drive at night waiting for the cat's slight rustling, the glow from town lighting the sky to the north over the river. The river is dark, running silent and deep, far below the surfaces I have walked.

DECEMBER 16

A candle, somebody's string quartet on the radio, a strong fire in the woodstove. In this part of the world, at this season of the year, that's when the afternoon light is starting to fade and the whole of creation is drawing in for the night. It is my own deep need for this place of solitude and safety that I read in the thick layers of R's choices. When I trace the series of improbable and serendipitous moments that have led me to this moment, in this place, I find another word to say aloud: *grace*.

DECEMBER 19

I have just taken a cheese kolache off the wood-burning stove. I sit down by the window at the table with my coffee and bite into the bun, crisp and warm. Outside the big window here, under what I think is a juniper, sparrows and chickadees feed as a very fine snow begins. I adjust the two fires. Inky the cat sleeps curled up on the rocker and Murray the dog wanders from window to window, watching the birds at the feeders and the squirrels who raid them, smells for intruders, then stops to look at me with pleading eyes. "Go lay down by the fire and dry off," I tell him, but he prefers my feet. The Beethoven violin concerto on the radio. The woodpecker at the tree stump again.

I heard an interview with an artist on WSUI the other morning.

She said that she had had the great fortune to get some grant or another and had been able to live alone on some island. She went on to describe the sights outside her window, the mountainous expanse of conifers, the clouds across the sky, the bear on the picnic table, the drama of sunset—and the entire time, I was thinking, "I know *exactly* what she means, what she is feeling."

I have only one week left here. I pack up the work I have been doing, turn to the work of leaving, reaching back for all that I am losing. All I really know is that this is a place that somehow feeds me, and that I have already grafted myself to it, this room, with fire and dog and violin, this road, this river, with eagle and snow, bend and current.

DECEMBER 21

Earlier this morning, when I was with Murray walking along the road, an eagle flew off downriver, which pulled from me a deep intake of breath, of both startle and awe. And then these words, unbidden, unknown, just came out of my mouth: "What have I done to deserve this? What have I done to deserve so much, not just one good thing, but such a surfeit?"

And there I was, walking the road, tears brimming over from a deep sadness I had not known I carried or had buried, not at all clear even what it was. I live with the echo of those questions for days and months, trying to name what burdens I have shouldered, what it is I find moving out into flight over the river, into the night, mingling with the geese flocks' murmuring, dissipating as fog lifts off the road after sunrise.

Leaving

EACH TIME I HAVE left the cabin on the river over the years I lived there—driven off the gravel road, checking the wall of gray dust that rises up behind me in the rearview mirror, bumped up onto the hard-top, past the League's lawn, the quarry gate, the stands of willow, the marsh and cornfields, navigated the potholes over the railroad tracks, and finally turned out onto old 218 heading not toward Hills but right, north—I am like the child in the back seat of a car, turned to the rear window, toward a receding figure, the cord that attaches to her breathing stretched, shredded, gone. I feel not as if I am being sent away or banished but that something is being torn from my hands, which are left extended, reaching, aching.

My throat aches. I drive on. By the time I am nearing Kalamazoo in Michigan, the four lanes of I-94 are straight and slightly elevated, heading due east where the full moon, I know, is due to rise. Due to rise, I know, because six hours behind me, if I turn onto Izaak Walton Road, the moon will just be cresting the trees. As I bump over the railroad tracks and potholes, I will sight it, huge and luminous, giving the cornfield day shadows, the rising heads of the deer in the stubble backlit, the road a cast of silver. The moon should be rising, but on the road passing Kalamazoo I cannot see it, and I am bereft.

PART II

WIND ⋏ WOOD ⋏ MEMORY

Memory believes before knowing remembers. Believes longer than recollects, longer than knowing even wonders.

—WILLIAM FAULKNER, *Light in August*

There are two spiritual dangers in not owning a farm. One is the danger of supposing that breakfast comes from the grocery, and the other that heat comes from the furnace.

—ALDO LEOPOLD, *A Sand County Almanac*

On the walls 1

OVER THE FIREPLACE, A large oval mirror, horizontally framed in light oak.

In a glass box to the right of the fireplace mantel, a collection of butterflies, moths, and bugs, most with tattered wings, pinned to white paper.

Framed things all around the front room, in every space, high up on the walls and tiered sometimes one above another.

A 1944 calendar, the top half a sepia photograph of a koala bear.

A small, old black-and-white photograph of a mountain peak, taken from a neighboring mountain peak. On the bottom left, someone has hand-printed in white, "Mt. Baker from Shuksan."

A faded Japanese print of chrysanthemums on a dark-gray background. Only hints remain of pink in the petals and green in the leaves.

Near the woodstove, two prints of birds, in the style of Audubon, faded.

Above the cherry sideboard, a watercolor—also faded—of a windswept prairie, a house far in the background, distant hills behind that, and a lot of white space.

A dark oak framed print next to the back door. A woman seated on a stone wall, in a long white dress, early nineteenth century, with baby-blue bow at empire waist, her light-brown hair up in a bun. She is strumming a guitar or lute, looking at a rowboat at her feet. The moon is large and bright. Like the others, this too is so old or faded that there's no color other than grayed blues, grayed browns, and gray off-white.

The cabin

IT WAS KATE KLAUS, I think, who told me it had once belonged to an old woman with a farm, who befriended R and gave it to her almost twenty years ago. Originally a simple hunting cabin, with no plumbing or electricity, it is long and narrow, a stone fireplace at its north end and leaky windows almost to the floor lining each long side. It sits low to the ground, rooted deep. Later additions branch off at successive angles. A kitchen, bathroom, and small sleeping room, with higher ceilings and knotty pine paneling. Behind that, another room, added even later, leading outside to a large square back deck. It's like the forts we used to build as children, the first room constructed with castoff lumber, then the box from a new refrigerator, then another smaller box, like a maze, like a homesteader's cabin. In this cabin, you can sit in the first room and through the wall of windows take in the river on one side, the gardens and woods on the other. You can sit in the first room on the cushioned wicker couch, look past raised flower beds and rows of young trees to the dirt road and the river, and beyond, to the woods on the other side of the river.

The front door is on that end, next to the stone fireplace. From the door, you come into an arctic entry, which works like an air lock to lessen the frigid temperature a little bit. There's barely room enough— if you are carrying bags of groceries or an armful of wood—to turn around to close the outer door before opening the inner one.

The fireplace insert provides the only heat in that room. Heat from the small furnace or the woodstove in the other room, two steps higher, never makes it to this original part of the cabin. The kitchen walls are lined with antique stoneware and utensils. Two cottage windows open inward, straight out of a fairy tale. There are no storm windows, nothing to keep winter air from billowing in through gaps between window and frame and around the glass where large chunks of glazing have long ago dislodged.

In the inner sitting room, there's a table, sideboard, and rocking chair. Sometime after the 1993 flood, R raised the ceiling, put in a new fan and new carpet. A wood-burning stove is set in the corner on a half shell of brick, two brick walls behind it, small bits of shell and pottery embedded in the mortar. The other two walls are heavy pine planks; a single row of bookshelf lines one wall beyond my reach. Many of the books are the same as ones on my bookshelves in Michigan.

"What's it like?" Kate asks me. "We've never seen it." Over dinner, she and Carl tell me bits and pieces of R's history, nothing firm, mostly gleaned from inferences, enough to be suggestive only. "I think the woman owned a farm elsewhere or a place in town, and just gave this to her," Kate says, "contents and all." At the time I think, If only I knew someone like that.

Much later, I set out to try to follow the traces of ownership through public records, in heavy deed and transfer books in the Johnson County Recorder's and Auditor's Offices and on color computer printouts from the County Assessor's websites. I visit cemeteries, dig through old newspapers for obituaries, correlate decades' worth of city directories and phone book listings. In the end, I realize I may very likely have followed a wrong thread, been misled by Kate's memory. In the end, after I have lived in R's place on and off over seven years, I realize I've shaped a story beyond memory and record, based more on what I've lived with day to day—things my hands touch and my feet walk over, the tools in the shed, utensils in the kitchen, broken pottery under the comfrey—than on legal descriptions and recorded deeds.

The gift

THIS IS THE STORY I tell myself about the giving and the giver, the cabin and how it came to R. The more I recite it to myself, recognize a portion of it in some crockery on a cupboard shelf or bit of old hardware, or add a bit of connecting tissue, the more I believe its truth.

She was a wife, finished high school, never aspired to degrees beyond that. But she imagined a great deal more. Things on the walls suggest it.

Someone sent "greetings and good wishes from Australia." She kept and framed it and hung it on a hook. In the small, old black-and-white photograph of sharply pointed mountains, a seated figure, back to the camera, gazes out across several snow-covered peaks.

A watercolor wash of koi next to it, also framed, red ideograms luring them like bait. She dreamed of other places, but never reached them.

A good woman, though not too good. Not bitter either, but I imagine that she kept an edge. Probably her children interested her more than her husband did. Maybe the stingy moments of play they were allowed reminded her.

There were chores; she was a farmwife. But I imagine her alone for most of her life. Whether by death or betrayal, he was gone, but I don't imagine he ever had much presence in her life anyway.

She looked nothing like the young woman in another framed print on the wall, seated on water's edge, dressed for a Jane Austen novel, gauzy white with a sash high at the waist. The moon repeats in the water; the background is dark, the frame is dark oak. And so I imagine her reading Keats, not quite dreaming of such a scene but yearning for something she could not name or put a finger on. Instead, she is out in the back among the chickens, bending in her rigidly tended garden to slice off cabbageheads, yank pole beans.

With few words and linens carefully mended and folded, she managed. And held on to a certain tightness around the mouth, a bit of hardness in her voice.

I like to think of her in simple clothes, cotton prints tied at the waist, plain cloth coats and plain white gloves only when she had to. But always something of her own—some small thing, something not always noticeable, a piece of defiance or exuberance. Pale-pink silk underdrawers. A bit of southwestern turquoise on a chain or a hat pin. An orange rayon scarf around a wide-brimmed straw hat. Not just sherry at night before bed but maybe also a cigar.

There is a little-known painter from South Dakota, Harvey Dunn, related by marriage to the Laura Ingalls Wilder family. His painting, *The Prairie is My Garden*, hangs in the museum collection at the University of South Dakota, and on her wall. It has the sweep of prairie and the composed perspective of a more famous painting by Andrew Wyeth, *Christina's World*—the one of a young woman crawling on the ground, reaching back into the picture's depth, away from the painter and toward a cabin made small by distance. In this other, the woman faces front, cabin and farm buildings in the distance behind her. She is staring off to the horizon, away from the cabin. One young girl-child plays near the stream by her feet; another hides behind her skirts, which are billowing, windswept like their hair. I see her in this woman, ramrod straight, a bit of dreaming, held to the ground by children but eyes drawn to a horizon of possibilities.

I imagine she lived in town and kept this place for something else. Not for use, but as a sign of possibility. Not as a secret but as a bit of extra, tucked away, a measure of reassurance.

I imagine her in later years, befriended by a flinty younger woman. A kindred spirit, in fact. Someone whose story—perhaps not even recent, not even close to the surface—is similar to her own in its fundamental unfairness. And because they are both hard workers, fiercely private and fiercely independent, they bend backs together in tending the sweeping curves of flower beds, carefully measured rows of herbs, leafy greens of many shades, swelling roots of dark flesh. I imagine it was slowly at first that she found herself giving to the other, first an apron, a trowel, a metal tackle box, a hoe, an iron gate, excess of irises. I imagine it was one or two small favors that led to the habit of spending time together, bent as often over china teacups or old-fashioneds as mounded rows of seeds.

And I can go on in this imagining, convincing myself this is the inevitable story. That as she straightened up, a little stiff, feet straddling the row of onions, she quietly mentioned her intention to give it all to the younger woman, to pass on the privacy, the tangible evidence as much of steadfastness as of rebellion. That the younger woman did not, as I most likely would have, overdo her thanks, but took the gift quietly, continued to pull weeds, turn earth, keep faith. Both of them knowing that the giving was easier than the receiving.

I imagine that this was not quickly followed by a deathbed, did not represent some eerie foretelling. That she simply knew this was the only sense to be made, that her sons would always be elsewhere, unable to understand what led her to hang on to the place for that long anyway. And that the contents that came with it—came to the younger woman even before death took away the companionship—would be cherished as well. Would be used even in brokenness, shards of teacup embedded in stone mortar, lost buttons finding a place among the gravel drive, milk pitchers with broken handles catching rainwater in the garden.

Because I have lived with the photographs and paintings on the walls, the broken teacups in the garden, the linens and silver in felt-lined drawers, this is the story I have embellished over the time I've lived here, a product of mapping my own regrets and desires onto the dusk air, the geese settling on the river's opposite bank, the hidden snags, the piney groves of the owl's dark and necessary silence. And because it is a story I have imagined, I also imagine a lingering illness.

Heart failure, perhaps, a slow weakening, a slowly descending frailty. In the carved-out spaces here in this place, pockets of shade, small caves of coolness under pine boughs, the pool of dappled light through splayed crab apple branches or beside the lilac hedge, a sadness lingers even with the abundance. It is sadness of separation.

I imagine her buried under some slab that her family chose, following a habit they never thought to reconsider. I imagine her spirit longing for the ground my felt-slippered feet walk at dusk, at dawn, reaching for a place she never lived, did not call home. And sometimes I realize her yearning is my own.

On the mantel

A ROSEWOOD BOX XYLOPHONE, the keys carved out of the middle of a single piece of wood.

Wooden Andean pipes, leather lashed.

A finger piano, graduated strips of metal on a hollow box, hand-crafted in a mosaic of cherry, walnut, oak.

A drum covered in shiny ball bearings, strung together, like river-splashed pebbles. You rub your hands on the covering to make the sound.

Three oval rattles, dark red, deep emerald, black enamel, painted with primary-colored flowers and geometric designs.

Hanging chimes, brass rods suspended from a dark wood frame. One of the rods missing.

The silence of an empty stone fireplace.

Sleeping with animals

BEFORE I CAME TO stay in the cabin on the river, I had not lived with a dog. When I came to live with Murray, I was forced out of doors each day, forced to pay attention. Because of Murray, every day I walked the road.

Back in Michigan, I had two cats. One was orange and fourteen years old, the other black and two years old. Each had white paws, a white V bib. I never let them out of doors.

Inky the cat was also black with white paws and a white bib. She spent a good deal of time outside around the cabin. R told me to keep her inside at night and when I went into town. If I called her name like this, she said—Inky-buy, Inky-buy—she would come. At night in bed, she curled up on my legs. Murray slept in a basket most of the day, or in front of the fire. At night, he sat by the side of the bed and silently, expectantly waited. R told me he would want to sleep on the bed and that I should let him. I had never slept with a dog. The first night, I could feel his patience like a laser even in the dark. I made room.

By the time I left the cabin in late December that first year, the attachments had thickened like viny undergrowth. Someone else was supposed to feed Murray and Inky between my departure and R's return. I had told her: "If you can't find anyone to take care of them when you go south again in January, I will keep them in Michigan."

I met her halfway, in Chicago, to get them from her, and for three months they lived with me and my two cats. Each found another to curl up with. In photos of the two black cats, you cannot tell them apart. In Lansing, I had to put a leash on Murray to teach him about sidewalks. The best days were when I could drive him to the cemetery, where he could run free. And where I would often see a hawk or owl as it flew from a cell tower, heading farther back into the woods along the interstate.

In April, R came to Michigan to pick up Murray and Inky. She bristled when I gave her all the details about the care I'd taken, the preferences and habits they'd developed with each other in my house, and when I took her to walk the cemetery.

And I, in my own ways, must have held on a little too long to the cords of attachment as I sent them back with her to the cabin on the river.

In the late fall, I received a box in the mail from R. Inside were her green felt clogs that I had worn while there, and a photograph of Murray at my house in Michigan, which I had sent to her in Belize. No words.

I cannot tell you how I knew, but I did. Nothing more was needed to let me know that R had taken Murray and Inky out of the country with her, and that I would never see them again.

On the walls 2

A POSTER, IN BRIGHT colors, of the Community Baboon Sanctuary in Belize. Varieties of monkeys climbing all over. Armadillos. Toucans, and other birds I cannot identify. And the same maroon-red flowers with seedpod centers, whatever they are, that appear in late spring on two bushes behind the cabin here.

Simple line drawings, flat and stylized, of several artifacts of ancient Belize. Diving God: a masked figure heading downward but looking straight ahead, legs like a frog, as if already swimming away. God of the Winds: another masked figure in side profile, taking a step, brace-lets on each ankle, fringe at one knee, robed with an animal, its head almost to the ground.

Covering the window on one back door, a black cloth, figures woven in white, yellow, red. Covering the window of the door that leads to the back deck, another piece of red cloth, woven with geomet-rical borders.

More framed drawings, this time in deep colors, of rural life in a Latin American village. Women carrying baskets, sorting fruit, cook-ing. A family, a village, a road to the fields, a parrot. In some, the red-and-orange sun hangs in the sky. In several, off to the side of the path to a little house, or surrounding the faces, so finely drawn and with such distinctive color, I recognize coleus, elephant's ear philodendron, caladium, yucca.

On the thin ledge above the bathroom window, postcards of crayon-colored fish, a coral reef. Tacked to the wall behind the water heater, more postcards. White sand beaches, a turquoise sea. Flamingos, parrots, birds of paradise, thatched roofs and palms, a canoe on a perfectly flat bay.

A parrot constructed of hammered silver foil. A phoenix of red feathers, the branch on which it sits delicately painted in white and pink.

Above the bathtub, a huge fan of coral. On other walls, more coral fans and branches of coral. Between the coral, a tropical fish styled in very thin wood veneer.

A collection of Belize stamps, the glass cracked, the frame simple. A faded color photograph of a door in the corner of a room, an empty window framing the bright sand, palms, sea.

And everywhere, strings of shells. Each string a single kind, different sized.

The space outside

THE ENTIRE SPACE OUTSIDE the cabin is a refuge—a mix of wild and shaped, chaos and planned, whimsical, haphazard, full of care and make-do. Its boundaries shield and shelter, cocoon and comfort. Like a mother's full skirt, a lover's encircling arms, a secret garden.

At the end of the gravel drive, hovering just outside the door, a short, scraggly cedar. On it hangs a birdhouse, wire sunflower seed feeder, hummingbird feeder, suet cage, twirling geometric assemblage of Popsicle sticks. Under it, the woodpile and a doghouse filled with gardening tools.

Close up against the cabin, in front of the windows, a wide juniper spreads itself. It carries snow heavily in its branches, where cardinals and nuthatches take refuge.

Along the road, the place is lined by a low stone wall, falling over in parts, and by trees—Scotch pines and crab apple, walnut, sycamore, oak, cottonwood, and hackberry, unfamiliar to me, but which I later learn makes a poor-quality burn. Inside the low wall, there are more stone walls, mortared with concrete, embedded with bits of shell, coins, broken pottery, all circumscribing bushes and ornamental trees.

On the other side of the road, next to the river and beneath another towering sycamore, a small turquoise house trailer, one of those old ones with rounded roof—a Serro Scotty Sportsman, its logo a little black Scotty dog. The door is locked, the curtains drawn. Vines have grown up and dried, tangled around the hitch, and the bottom has rusted out.

Closer to the river, two rusted chairs, a thick weathered plank set on concrete blocks, and in the middle an open fire pit, a mound of ash and charred wood.

Dried canes and thorny vines cover the propane tank along the side of the cabin. A chicken wire fence—the old kind, with half-moon tops—starts here, marking off what was once a garden and is now a mass of dried and matted brush.

In back of the cabin, a deck, a shed, a massive outdoor stone fireplace, and all around, every tree stump has been put to use—topped with a bird feeder or rusted tea kettle, cradling an ax blade or anchoring a fence. By the garden gate, a fifteen-foot stump, a ceramic sun face nailed to its middle, a broken glass pitcher at its foot.

Behind the shed, more white pines, planted after the flood in 1993, and beyond them, more massive walnut. A path takes me back among tangled brush and woods to a small clearing and evidence of another long-neglected garden plot in the dense tangle of vine and brush. I don't venture that far.

In the middle of the area out back, a boat oar stands upright, an upturned old metal milk crate below it, bird feeders suspended from brackets at its top. Later I learn that by the end of spring, the massive leaves of an old bed of comfrey have made dense shelter for rabbits, the blue pendulous flowers persistent and plentiful. By midsummer, it's all lying flat on the ground, a blanket mess.

Behind the back door on this oldest part of the cabin, right up against the cabin wall, an ancient and enormous trumpet vine, thick as a tree trunk and twice as tall as the cabin, is completely entwined through a twenty-foot TV antenna.

The property is full of attempts to mark space, to both tame and claim. What's wild, what's native, all of it appears to be creeping back toward the cabin, reaching in, covering, and taking over. Slowly blurring the boundaries between inside and outside.

Derecho

ON LABOR DAY WEEKEND that year, I come back to Iowa City for a brief visit. Based on what she's told me, I expect R to stay until early November, when it will start getting too cold. I drive out to see her one afternoon. It's sunny and hot, and the dust rises in a cloud behind my car as I leave the concrete of Izaak Walton Road and bump onto the dirt and gravel of Camino del Rio.

It looks the same, mostly, as when I left last December. I notice that the second cabin on the road is gone, the one where a black Lab was tied up day and night a year ago, on a rope that looked too short. The foundation is still there, and the doghouse, and a satellite dish, but the structure is not, leaving a clear sight line to the river. I continue on to R's place. Beside her driveway, the single-wide house trailer is also gone—the one she'd rented out to two guys last year, instructing me to collect the rent. Between its door and the road, a triangle of spruce had marked a sheltered front yard. Now grasses and shrubs have grown up in its place, covering any footprint the trailer had made.

I follow R into the cabin cautiously. For a year, I have held it all in memory, held it like blown glass, passing a finger over each contour, lingering, tracing again. It is like entering dreamscape. Any change, I am afraid, will break its spell for me.

She is talking about how she might just sell the place now. "Girl, don't you see that all the trees are gone? Look at it! All of them! Oh god, it just killed me!"

I look around, out back behind the pump house, in front to the road, then across the road to the river's edge, to the river's other side. I feel disoriented. I can't perceive any change, so strongly do I cling to the place in memory. But R's incredulity and the pain in her voice raise my doubt.

Then she grabs my wrist and starts pointing.

▲

On June 29, 1998, the National Weather Service was watching a storm work its way across Iowa. It wasn't expected to be very strong in the west, but to gather in intensity as it moved east. According to the National Climatic Data Center's "event record" for that day, "Supercell thunderstorms developed over central Iowa and rapidly intensified into a long squall line which raced southeast over eastern Iowa into central Illinois. . . . Straight-line winds from 60 to over 120 mph produced the most serious damage with these storms, and eight counties in eastern Iowa were declared disaster areas." What hit Iowa City between 1:30 and 3:00 p.m. that afternoon created damage that took the rest of the summer to clean up.

"You don't need a tornado to have a disaster, Johnson County residents learned Monday," begins one of the stories in the June 30, 1998, edition of the *Iowa City Press-Citizen*. On one side of that lead paragraph, a small box explains that "because of power outages in Iowa City Monday," the newspaper was printed in Davenport by the *Quad City Times*. To the left of that opening sentence is a photograph of several train cars dangling vertically off the Riverside Drive railroad bridge, dipping into the water below. Among the many buildings in Iowa City reported to have lost a roof was the Colonial Lanes bowling alley on Riverside Drive. Underneath the photograph are headlines for other stories inside: "Oxford Loses Fire Station to Wind"; "Hospital Area Flooded"; "Mobile Homes Heavily Damaged"; "Residents Help Each Other"; "Restoring Power May Take Days."

The National Climatic Data Center's event record describes the storm's effects in two single-spaced pages, including these facts. Across the county, sustained straight-line winds of 70 to 80 miles per hour ripped down trees, power lines, and windmills, and knocked over farm buildings, grain bins, and silos. About 30,000 acres of corn were destroyed in the main path of the storm, with widespread agricultural damage reported across the remainder of the county. The lost corn crop was valued at $5.5 million by US Department of Agriculture representatives. F. W. Kent Park near Tiffin was closed due to storm damage after thousands of trees in the 1,010-acre park were blown down. One rural electric company reported only 5 of 21 substations were left online after the storm. One utility company replaced over 450 poles and restored over 100 miles of wire downed by the storm. In rural Johnson County, 30 barns were destroyed, and more than 330 wooden sign posts were snapped by the wind. Across the county, 50 homes (most of them mobile homes) were destroyed. Approximately 100 families spent the night in emergency shelters.

The *Press-Citizen* was dominated for days afterward by stories of damage, cleanup, inconveniences, and delays, including the Iowa City Fourth of July celebrations and fireworks postponed because of flooding in City Park. It took days for power to be restored to many areas. On July 2, the paper reported that power company crews were finding "equipment damage so severe along some rear property lines that they spend twelve hours on a single pole." Some people were without power for a week or more.

It took even longer to clean up the trees and limbs littering streets and property all over the city and the rural parts of the county. Well into August, the paper was reporting that cleanup continued and that the city was offering free mulch at the landfill. It reported an estimated 25 percent of the county's tree stock was destroyed by the storm, noting that the figure was conservative. A local tree expert said it was closer to 50 percent of the city's tree stock, especially of the larger, older trees in City Park.

▲

It was three in the afternoon. A librarian at the University of Iowa told me she was working a reference desk in the main library that day. "You could hear the winds through vents, shaking everything," said Charlene, her voice and face taut with amazement even four years later. "They told all the staff up on the floors to come down to the basement." They didn't stay long, less time than with most tornado warnings, and she went back to work for the rest of the afternoon.

But when she left to go home that evening, walking up the hill to catch a bus, the first thing that caught her eye, she said, were all the enormous old trees on the Pentacrest that had been blown over. The bus ride took twice as long as normal because the driver couldn't go his regular route. Whole trees had fallen across Summit Street, "and he had to go this way and that, going way out of his way to get close to each stop along his route."

Charlene's husband works for MidAmerican Energy. He stayed on the job all the way through until 9:30 p.m. on Tuesday, came home to sleep for a few hours, then went back for another twenty-four-hour shift. It was that way all week. "We knew there was a storm coming across the state," he said. "One of our power substations had been switched out of service because of a bridge repair up by Tiffin. We were told to head out there to switch it back in, but we never made it because the storm hit first. And it took out the entire substation down by Hills. The damage up on the north and west sides of town was not nearly as bad as that south and east of town."

"When we went out to start fixing the Hills substation, headed down Sand Road and Old Highway 218, you could see all the trees downed all over on the south side of town, and they were all laying in the same direction," he said. "And if you go walk the trails up the big hill in Ryerson's Woods, you can still see all those trees even today, all laying in the same direction."

Tom Hansen, the emergency management coordinator for Johnson County, later told me, "I was on watch that day. It wasn't a tornado. It didn't show up on radar and it didn't touch down. But it started clear over by Wellman and took down everything."

According to the Storm Prediction Center's website, a derecho—from the Spanish word for "direct" or "straight"—is a widespread and long-lived windstorm that is associated with a band of rapidly moving showers or thunderstorms. This use of the word "derecho" was coined by Dr. Gustavus Hinrichs, a physics professor at the University of Iowa, in a paper published in the *American Meteorological Journal* in 1888.

According to meteorologist Jeff Haby, "The length of time the severe winds last can be particularly damaging. While a severe thunderstorm may produce severe convective wind gusts that last for several minutes at a point location, derecho wind can last thirty minutes or longer." His website details climatological maps of significant derecho events that have caused severe damage and casualties. In July 1995, for example, a derecho swept from Montana through Ontario, Canada, to New England. A derecho that traveled from western Iowa to the coast of Maryland on July 4, 1980, caused 73 fatalities. An "unbelievable natural event" in 1999 in the Boundary Waters Canoe Area Wilderness leveled trees in a swathe more than 30 miles long. One million acres of forest were damaged by a 1995 derecho in the Adirondacks. Severe straight-line winds in July 1995 damaged 129,000 acres in a swath from Detroit Lakes to Bemidji, Minnesota, and 113,000 acres in a path south of Grand Rapids, Michigan. In places, virtually every tree was leveled.

▲

On July 8, the *Press-Citizen* reported that the county was trying to assess damages from the storm, to reduce hassles for residents so they could get on with repairing and replacing property damaged by the storm. The county assessor, talking about the annual requirement that property owners report value changes in their property, said that downed trees would not be figured into property values: "They're not an issue. We don't add or deduct value for [trees]."

On Friday, July 17, the Federal Emergency Management Agency (FEMA) opened a center in Iowa City for the people who had suffered damage from the June 29 storm. It received 4,213 applications for disaster assistance. The *Press-Citizen* reported that "Barbara Wiese of Oxford came to the center Friday afternoon to inquire about extensive damage on her two-and-a-half-acre property. She said she had spent a couple thousand dollars for helpers to clear damage caused by the loss of about 30 trees."

In yet another *Press-Citizen* story on the "trouble with trees," Tom Hansen is reported as saying, "With trees, nobody realizes the value of them—until they're down."

▲

At the cabin on Camino del Rio, trees three and four feet in diameter lay flat alongside the driveway and back behind the pump house, their root balls exposed, webs and crevices still raw. Several others of the sixty- and eighty-foot trees that had shaded and sheltered the cabin had been cut off midsection, their top halves dangling or already cut and split. Across the river, the tops of all the trees had been sheared off. Because everything was still green, and because two months' growth had filled it in a bit, it was possible not to notice the damage immediately. At least, that's the way I explained to myself how it was that I had driven down the road and seen only what I remembered.

R was beside herself with loss. She spoke again about maybe finally selling. After the 1993 flood, FEMA had offered to buy out each of the owners on the road. "When the ninety-nine-year lease is up, the county will take it over anyway, so maybe I should just take the money now." Her voice was hardening. Requests for new zoning were being brought by the sand and gravel company—hadn't I noticed all the dump trucks going back and forth? "I can't stay here anymore," she said. "That storm just took it all."

I, on the other hand, was like a lover who grasps at any straw, who clings to each frayed thread of a connection to what was, grateful for even a few moments of presence. It was a desperation entirely defined by so much of my past: the loss several years before of my first house in Iowa City, whatever even older losses that had touched, the place in my heart that living in the cabin had opened again. And the fear that once again I would be left empty handed. In this rarified air, I could barely breathe. I hardly noticed the trees.

A month later, the box with the clogs and photo was at my front door.

PART III

SKY ⋏ ROAD ⋏ BLOOD

When we are able to keep company with our own fears and sorrows,
we are shown the way to go; our own parched lives are watered
and the earth becomes a greener place.

—ELIZABETH O'CONNOR, *Cry Pain, Cry Hope*

i thank You God for most this amazing
day: for the leaping greenly spirits of trees
and a blue true dream of sky; and for everything
which is natural which is infinite which is yes

—E. E. CUMMINGS, FROM *XAIPE*

There are some who can live without wild things, and some who cannot.

—ALDO LEOPOLD, *A Sand County Almanac*

January

THE PHONE IS RINGING just as I pull into the dark drive and unlock the cabin door at a little after six at night, three years later. It's my brother calling from Los Angeles to find out if I've made it safely from Michigan. I have left the car running, fully loaded with my dog, three cats, computer, books, kindling, linens, pillow, coats, boots, and clothes enough for six months. I need to find out what's inside before I let any of the animals loose. It's cold and dark, and I'm exhausted. Cheryl and Bill, who rented the cabin from R until early December, had told me there was evidence of mice. When I called them a few days ago to ask about last-minute details, they offered to set a few traps, because the place had been sitting empty for a month. They also came by this morning to turn up the heat and leave the key for me, hidden on a hook in the tiny entryway.

I find two mousetraps complete with carcasses, and mouse droppings everywhere in the kitchen. There's not a single surface that doesn't have some evidence of their activities. One cabinet under the sink has clearly been a gathering spot: the odor spills out when I open the door, the pressed board shelving soaked and bloated with urine and feces.

I clean one counter. Then, over the iced path, I start hauling in the contents of my car, what I have estimated will be enough to take me from midwinter through early summer teaching and living in the cabin on the edge of the river.

When I learned seven months ago that I would be invited to teach here at the university, I called R to ask if there was any chance her place would be available to rent just for six months. I had not known what to make of the clogs and photograph sent to me with no note. But she answered immediately, "When do you want to come? Can you come now? You can live here anytime you want." No, I explained, I had my teaching commitments in Michigan until December. I could only be in Iowa from January until July at the latest. "Well, there's some people from Alaska I was going to rent to—you know I don't like to do that—you know I would much rather have you here. When will you come? I'll tell them they have be out by December."

Later when I spoke to her again, she told me, "Use anything you want. You know where everything is. And check over everything when you get there—if they haven't cleaned well enough for you, let me know. I have a damage deposit so if it's not OK for you, just let me know. You know how I do things, you know how I am."

When I spoke to Cheryl and Bill, they sounded relieved to be moving out even before they were supposed to. Thinking I'd never seen the place, they tried to warn me about what to expect. "It's pretty primitive. Plan on bringing your own things—I wouldn't use anything here that's going to touch your body or your food. And it's pretty cold."

I knew what to expect, I said.

▲

I spend all of the next day unpacking and cleaning, and still there's so much more to do. But I also have to get to my office, to unpack books and prepare materials for classes, which begin Monday. There's no firewood, and I realize I don't know whether the chimneys to the woodstove and the fireplace have been cleaned at all in the past three years that R has not been living here. Nothing has been done to make the cabin ready for winter. The storm windows are still not in place.

There's no plastic on those windows that leak. Even without the wind, icy air pours in from gaps I can see through all around the frames. I find a dead mouse under the stovetop and one in the broiler tray. Both are old and dried. I find an old blanket frozen in the ice and snow outside the front door, but no snow shovel. I trek to the Goodwill to buy up tins for storing all my food. Since I don't know where the mice have traveled, I wash everything with bleach. The silverware in its tray is sealed in an extra-large ziplock baggie in a drawer, but a small bit of one corner has been chewed off. I can't find a toaster, an iron, a pot to boil water in. I keep most things in the refrigerator and freezer. I fall into bed spent and aching each night.

Because the old front part of the cabin is about a foot lower than the other rooms, and because it has no heat ducts, it never warms up. The back room—the one with the closets—has no heat duct either, and R has instructed me to keep the door between it and the bedroom closed in order to save heat. The door is oversized and large, half of it glass, and gets stuck on the sill when it's closed. Sometimes I can't get it open at all, but when I do, I enter a room that must be no more than forty degrees. My clothes, when I extract them, are as cold as my car seat in the early morning.

The cats are drawn to the many windows and any perch for viewing the dramas outside. Next to the three front windows in the main room, the branches of the fat juniper, its fullness spread low to the ground, are often dancing with chickadees and cardinals. Right up against the back window, in the dense branches of another juniper and the thick woody branches of the ancient trumpet vine interwoven with the twenty-foot antenna, birds pop in and out, settling for the night. Beyond, on poles and in each tree, there are bird feeders of every kind and at every height. Dried seedpods in sheaves of prairie grasses and small pockets of shrubby cover draw congregations. Woodchucks, rabbits, and deer migrate through. At night, all the animals sit hunched and alert, staring out into the blackness of the bare back window, blank to me but apparently not to them.

On the second day, I see the two younger cats sitting in the woodstove room, eyeing the brick ledge above and behind it. Callie needs no more than a glance; Emmy stares and measures, measures and wiggles, stares and repositions. Soon both of them have leaped to the woodstove, scaled the brick wall, figured the angle for another leap from its ledge, around the stovepipe, to the top of the heat ducts. Inching across to the end closest to the small furnace, they sleep or watch.

Woodstoves

IN THE LOW FRONT room, a Lopi Answer woodstove is set into the opening of the old fieldstone fireplace. It has a glass door, a shiny steel handle on the left. Vents and grills are all around the black cast-iron body. When I manage the burning badly, dark-orange residue builds up on the inside of the glass door.

In the kitchen, two steps up, the freestanding woodstove is a Resolute. It has a solid front that opens like an oven door. You can leave this door down, put a rounded wire mesh grill across the opening, and watch the fire as if it were an open fireplace. This, of course, defeats the purpose.

On the top, you load the wood by lifting another door. Or set a cast-iron pot of water on it, the evaporation countering the drying effect of the very hot stove and the pipe that runs up the brick corner wall.

Each of the two stoves in the cabin requires a slightly different operation—or at least so it seemed to my inexperience the first time I listened to R's directions. All I took in was that it could backfire: there are ways to screw it up and those ways can be dangerous. There was some balance to be achieved between air and airtight—close the damper but only after something happens, don't open the door, or open it only after you've closed or opened something else, pulled this lever in or out, turned this one clockwise or counter.

I call around and find someone to deliver a cord of wood, which turns out to be wet through and through, having sat out in a field under snow cover for months.

I scavenge for kindling. I walk the road picking up downed branches, breaking them in manageable pieces, carrying them back.

I have the chimneys cleaned. The man who does it, whose name I found in the free circular that came in the mail, says the Lopi required a bend in order to be fitted into the fieldstone fireplace, and that this is not an efficient arrangement.

There is a deep quiet in the cabin without the motors and fans of the small furnace. It provides enough heat to keep the pipes from freezing when no one's here and the security that if there is no wood, no one will freeze. I prefer the woodstoves. I prefer the sounds of burning wood. I am drawn to the rhythm of tending the fire, getting up periodically to check it, poke it, add to it. The rhythm gives my mornings a pattern, my evenings curled up reading a focus.

Too many times, I start the fire, close the door, sit back, and find the box filling with yellow-white smoke, which soon starts seeping out the vents and grills into the cabin. A whiff of wood smoke wakes me at 3:00 a.m. In that strange half-awake state—when whatever you are thinking seems perfectly clear at the same time that it seems like the slowed motion of swimming up through darkened water—I believe I will be asphyxiated in my sleep.

It is early evening on a night that is once again supposed to see sub-zero wind chills. I fill the Lopi with logs, let them burn for about a half hour, then close down the damper. I struggle to keep the cabin warm with these two wood-burning stoves, struggle to keep enough supply of wood, struggle to deal with not-quite-cured-enough wood, or wet wood, or really soft crappy wood. There is abundant evidence that I really do not know what I'm doing.

I try to understand and learn. I drive out to the Ralston Creek store that sells wood-burning stoves and ask advice. I study the photocopied pages the salesman gives me.

The basic principle of a wood-burning stove is simple: a cast-iron box is heated, the cast iron holding and shedding the heat so that the room fills with its warmth. The good stoves have a catalytic combustor that burns off toxic gases before they go up the chimney. Or they are designed to enable a secondary combustion process by having a second air intake, which also helps burn off the gases. As wood burns, it releases not only gases but tar and charcoal and carbon, stuff that doesn't exactly improve the quality of air. It isn't until the fire reaches six hundred degrees that it starts burning off that stuff.

The names are heavy like the iron. Answer. Resolute. Vermont Castings. The handles and levers are definite in their positions and take a bit of heft to move. Vermont Castings is the most airtight, I'm told. It is also the only company that makes top loaders anymore. All of them come with ceramic glass doors now.

Fire burns front to back in the stoves. There is an art to laying, loading, and moderating the fire, and to operating the damper handle. It's not the same as building a campfire or using an open fireplace.

I am given these directions: To lay a fire, use more crumpled newspaper than you think can possibly fit. Pile kindling on top. Then layer successively thicker logs. The idea is to have enough flame and heat to get small logs burning and thereby establish a good mass of coal. This is what keeps the largest logs burning. Without enough white and red coals beneath the grill, the flames will die and the logs will only smolder.

To start the fire, first take a piece of newspaper, light it, and hold it up under the flue. This heats the cold air that has settled in the chimney and establishes a rising air current. This, I am assured, will keep the smoke from backing into the room.

I never quite learn it all. I use too much wood. I burn too much wet and green and soft wood. Too many times, the cabin still fills with smoke.

Nevertheless, when I get it to work right, it is an immensely satisfying thing. The heat is plentiful and dry. It penetrates something in me deep and long closed.

When I was searching for a house to buy in Michigan, insisting on a fireplace, I rejected all those with woodstoves; I ignored people as they started talking about efficiency. I insisted on being able to see the fire, to reach easily into the flame. Yet by the time I have lived with the stoves for a month, I cannot imagine any other arrangement, the silence so full, the whisper of the fire one with the river and geese.

Massacre at the cabin, or Where's the carcass?

ONE NIGHT, SNUG UNDER the down comforter with Ollie the Old, I found myself slowly swimming up out of a deep sleep to sounds of Callie meowing—a sound at a lower pitch, more guttural than usual. It took me a long time to realize it was her, and somehow I came to realize it was not a sound of distress but of contented playing. I don't know how I knew this. I was just annoyed, thinking, Why now?? and I wasn't going to get up. But it went on and on, and finally I remembered that when the animals are making sounds or being alert, I should pay attention even if I can't immediately perceive the reason. So I got up, turned the light on, and yes, sure enough, she was happy to see me, because there in the middle of the floor in the woodstove room was a mouse carcass. Thank you very much. Pick it up, dispose of it. Back to bed.

The next night, I became aware of Callie staring intently at the stove in the kitchen—her little head darting back and forth. Now, I'd known that mice are back there, even though I hadn't seen any droppings since I cleaned up that first week. I knew the population wasn't limited to the two who had had their necks snapped for my arrival, and although I hoped the others had moved out when they saw the carnage, I knew that was probably wishful thinking. I was moderately happy to simply wipe the counters down with bleach every morning, check the two remaining traps, check the drawer for droppings, and keep all edibles in the refrigerator or in jars and tins. If they would only stay out of my way, I'd refrain from setting any more traps.

So I took Aggie the dog out for a walk down the road to the mail-boxes and left Callie to do her thing. Mind you, I had no idea what "her thing" was, because she had come to me only six months before, a very young cat. When we came back, she was positioned by the dog crate, hyperalert. When I pulled the crate away from the wall, Callie pounced and with the mouse in her mouth, stalked off into the big room growling, as if to say, *Nobody* come near me, this is *mine*.

This was followed by twenty minutes of Callie slinking from under-neath one chair to the next, sometimes letting the mouse loose so it could try to escape, recapturing it, tossing it around. And there I was, trying to figure out how I could possibly intervene—because I know from scars on my own hands that if I try to take something out of her mouth, she simply clamps down with strength and determination far beyond what you'd expect from a six-pound house pet. After roughly twenty-five minutes, it was dead, but she continued to play with it, tossing it in the air. I sat in the rocker in the other room, waiting. At long last, she came toward me, mouth empty.

But I could not find the carcass anywhere. Nothing. Nada. No bits or pieces or residue. In response to my long-distance frantic phone call the next morning, my vet said she ate it. Every little bit of it.

So OK, she ate it, I tell myself—but I don't want her bloody mouth or paws near me. All I can think of is that old B. Kliban cartoon that I used to find so disgusting but funny: "Love to eat them mousies, bite their little heads off, nibble on their tiny feet." You could buy an apron stenciled with the cartoon. When Callie had the mouse by the foot, still alive, and was dragging it around, I made the mistake of meeting its eyes. There was nothing funny about it. My heart hurt.

I don't want the mice in the house. But I don't want them dead. I don't want them to suffer. I don't want to think of their terror—and yet I can't help that I do, that my body recoils with the image, and I don't know what to do with the way my body will continue to react to the visual memory. It will be years before I learn the skill of interrupt-ing that connection, the memory followed by a recoil in my chest. It will be years before it occurs to me that my wholehearted desire to protect and provide safe shelter for small creatures—for all creatures—is connected to my own small self that experienced the home into which I was born as a terrifyingly unsafe place, where my hurts, my terror, the emotional and physical violations that threaded through those years were unspoken, unacknowledged, just the given order of things.

The next night, 1:30 a.m. I hear a pounce. I know what it is. I stay in bed and do not turn on the light. I listen to a replay of the soundtrack from the night before, without the visuals. In the morning, there is no evidence.

Bald eagles

THE FIRST TIME I lived in the cabin on the river and walked the road, I thought the bald eagle that dropped out of a tree and into flight upriver was a gift, a spirit or guide, and yes, though I am embarrassed to admit it, a sign that I belonged here. This time when I got here, the first week in January, I realized there was not one eagle but two. And then one morning last week, four. And today, a single bald eagle sitting atop a tree precisely opposite, staring across the river into the long windows, at me, for an hour. Each time I see one, like the very first time I walked down the road with Murray, I am stricken, caught. There are no words. Just an uplift of breath, my diaphragm pulled outward, reaching for something I cannot name.

A month later, as I let Aggie out to relieve herself one last time before I jumped in my car and headed into town to teach, one of the eagles flew low past us, then up to a tree branch. I put Aggie inside, got my camera, and walked a bit down the road. I stood and watched four of them flying the length of the river. One buzzed the geese. They flew at my eye level, maybe twenty-five yards away. I had no idea how huge and fast they are when they want to get somewhere, when they're not—as in most video footage—simply soaring. And still I struggle to grasp a sense of the size and bulk of one.

Another morning, I saw an eagle land on a tree on our side of the river, down toward the end of the road. I corralled Aggie, made her stay with me, and walked slowly toward it. It let me get pretty close— about twenty feet—before it took off. We watched it circle and head for the woods across the river. Then we turned and headed home, away from the direction where the Doberman lives, the one dog Aggie hasn't decided whether to ignore or like. Probably it's me who hasn't decided. I've kept her inside when a pack of dogs parades by every morning, in single file along the road.

As we walked back, I saw her chomping on something again but this time I was close enough to grab her, pry open her mouth, and retrieve a piece of a fish head. I realize then that the eagles are finding fish in the icy water and I don't need to worry that they will go after my dog. I am relieved, but not yet able to laugh at myself. Later I check in the Golden bird guide and find out that although the wing-span of bald eagles is eighty inches—more than six and a half feet—they weigh only nine and a half pounds, lighter than Aggie by several pounds.

The open river. The fish. That's why they are here.

The owl

I FIRST HEAR IT in early February at the window facing the woods, away from the river.

We all are drawn to the center of gravity around the tumbling, snapping, gently hissing fireplace that warms the uninsulated, leaky front room. In the evening, I sit lengthwise on the wicker couch, snug under a woolen blanket the color of new leaves, cradling the old cat like a suckling child or a swaddled infant, my back to the large window, reading. I don't mind that there's no covering on the window—no curtains or blinds—because there's no one back there, nothing to hide from. But there are times I have the distinct sense of being watched, of creatures who know when I get up and walk to the stove to heat water for tea or add a log, who take note even when I turn a page.

The evening moves to the rhythm of burning logs, turning pages, adding logs, settling back to silence. Into that silence comes a sound I cannot place, a sound that persists, then ceases, then starts up again. It's very close to the window sometimes, loud enough that I feel its vibrations. At first, I vaguely brush it away, as if it's antenna wire rattling against the house siding. It takes me several evenings to pay attention, to listen, to acknowledge that it's something worth listening to. Night after night, as soon as it gets dark, I hear it behind me, over and over, for long minutes. Only then do I realize it is not inanimate—it is a creature, and it is very, very close by. Perched in the dense juniper next to the window or the gnarled trumpet vine and antenna beside it.

Or maybe in the young white pine out beyond the chimney, its call pressing heavily on the windowpane, echoing in my blood, pulsing hard against my rib cage.

Each night, I listen, astonished, but it takes several more nights before it occurs to me that I might try to find out what it is. With no experience and no firsthand knowledge, my mind runs through TV possibilities. Coyote? Wolf? What else would be making sounds—*ooo ooooo ooooo*—late at night? Several more nights before I think, half a question, It could be an owl.

One morning at dawn, Aggie and I walk along the road. Down out of a tree and across the edge of the pony pasture floats something large, as big as the eagles across the river. But silent. With the road and fields in darkness and the sky barely light, I see only silhouette, a rounded head. Not eagle, crow, or turkey vulture.

I start trying to find out what kind of owl. I dig out a bird identification book, look at habitat maps, and read descriptions of the calls for all the owls common in this area. Words on a page just don't help. I can eliminate some but cannot definitively match any to what I've been hearing. I'm moderately confident it's not a barn owl, which "does not hoot, but has a soft ascending wheezy cry." And I'm hesitant about whether what I hear could be a short-eared owl, which "barks during breeding season" but is "otherwise silent." The great horned owl's "call is typically 4–7 low hoots," and so the next night I count, but I'm just not sure. Is what I hear "low"? The barred owl, I read, "typically hoots 8 times, 4–7 series/min." How do I tell the difference between the great horned and the barred? It's certainly not the western screech-owl's "4–10 short low-pitched whistles," but how would I distinguish between that and the northern saw-whet's "long series of short whistles"?

Nothing comes even close to the way the sounds on the other side of the huge black window become as heavy as a fist, as near as breathing. I know I should call back. I know that even from behind a double layer of windows I would be heard. I know it is that close. I hold the cat. I hold my breath.

Each night, it begins again. It is knocking on the window, it is searching out night's movements, it is calling me out into the oak woods. I step outside, glue my back to the door and wait. Wait for my eyes to adjust and my breathing to settle, for silence from the house to convince wildlife to return to business. With other birds and animals, this often works, but now there is always only silence from the tree. I scan the branches for anything silhouetted against the spread of stars or clouds. Nothing. Five minutes after I'm back inside settled under the blanket, it starts again.

The students in my graduate class are reading Aldo Leopold's *A Sand County Almanac*, a book that begins by following the tracks of small creatures in the snow, who rely on its cover for safety. The tracks lead to a bloody patch "encircled by a wide-sweeping arc of owl's wings." When I hear the owl, I keep Aggie inside. When I release the mice, I scan the tree branches above, then look down and see them to safety.

I come upon Scott Russell Sanders's essay "Listening to Owls." He writes about going out before dawn on a freezing winter solstice with a friend who can perfectly imitate owl calls. They crouch under trees, on the sides of hills, calling and shivering and waiting for barred, screech, and great horned. Sanders writes what I have already learned: bird books will tell you what an owl call sounds like, but whatever the books say bears no resemblance to what your flesh hears when the owl calls. He gives me some words from his own bird book for the barred owl's call: "Who cooks for you, who cooks for you all?" That night again I listen, carefully, but not one of the sounds reverberating the windowpane is any more "cooks" than "hoo" or "hoot" or "who."

▲

Late one Sunday afternoon, I am outside with a guy I've hired to chop wood from among the downed trees on the property. As the sun dips below the tree line across the river, I hear the owl, but from off across the woods, not close. I ask the guy, a farmer from a neighboring town, what kind it is, and he says, "I guess it's just a barn owl—what else is there?"

In that moment, I understand something about myself. My long-practiced, learned response to the dysfunction of my early life is to believe that the more information I have, the more I feel reassured I can handle the world around me. No doubt it accounts for why I was drawn to academic work. I go to books when I want to understand something. I know there are more kinds of owls than just that one, and I know that there is a way to find out which is which. To me, it matters. But it matters for no reason affecting my daily life and work—not because it's threatening my livelihood or property, not because I need to hunt or count or protect. It matters simply because I want to know who inhabits this place, what sort of life orders and textures it.

At the same time, I am also enough on the margins of that bookish community to know that what's in a book often misses or ignores the kind of knowledge that's passed hand to hand, in the fields or trenches or on the line. I naively assume a farmer will have knowledge that books render so imperfectly, that, as someone who spends time outside in the woods and fields, he will have this knowledge from a better source. Yet I am unfamiliar enough with this other world of outdoor work that it doesn't occur to me this farmer might not have this particular bit of knowledge. Because he, too, does not need it—it's not necessary for his livelihood and it doesn't threaten his property, nor is it something he wants to hunt or count or protect.

In this edge place, place knowledge falls between the cracks in the ecology of rural landscapes. A rancher in Montana will tell you a good deal about wolves, arguing consequences and facts with wildlife biologists, and my suburban neighbor will tell me about snakes in her yard because she hates being surprised by them among her tomatoes, but the owl isn't in anybody's way. And so no one pays attention to its disappearance from the vicinity as trees are felled for development and profit.

▲

But I am paying attention. I am paying attention because I cannot *not*—because the call each night pulls at my chest, pulls me out of myself, out the cabin door.

The next evening, I stand on the road, listening to the owls calling one another across the river—one on this side calls, a pause, then the other side of the river responds. This goes on for a long time.

Finally one day, I find OwlPages.com. For each of the twenty-seven snapshots of North American owls, I read about size, markings, preferred habitat, hunting, mating and breeding habits, mortality, and range, with another dozen photographs of the particular species in various settings, poses, and light. For each owl, under the section headed "Voice," the words used to describe the call are underlined and highlighted, a link to a voice recording.

I begin making my way through the photos systematically, clicking on each link. And finally there it is—the exact sound I've been listening to every night. I keep punching the link for the barred owl over and over, my blood responding, calling back. I send emails to friends across the country: "Go to https://www.owlpages.com/species/strix/ varia and you can hear exactly what's outside my window out here!" The word description of the call is more helpful, more accurate than any other resource I've found, before or since:

The Barred Owl is a highly vocal Owl giving a loud and resounding "hoo, hoo, too-HOO; hoo, hoo, too-HOO, ooo" which is often phrased as "Who, cooks, for-you? Who, cooks, for-you, all?" - The last syllable drops off noticeably. Like some other Owl species, they will call in the daytime as well as at night. The calls are often heard in a series of eight, then silence, when the Owl listens for a reply from other Owls. Other calls include "hoo-hoo, hoo-WAAAHH" and "hoo-WAAAHHH" used in courtship. Mates will duet, but the male's voice is deeper and mellower. Many other vocalisations are made which range from a short yelp or bark to a frenzied and raucous monkey-like squall.

Once I know that it's a barred owl, I begin searching and reading insatiably. The Golden field guide tells me its wingspan is forty-four inches. Another book tells me it's twenty-one inches long. I learn that when barred owls begin to mate in February, they respond readily to calls. I learn that amateur naturalist Benjamin Smith Barton was the first to publish, in 1799, a description of a barred owl. I learn that it is also known as northern barred owl, swamp owl, striped owl, hoot owl, eight hooter, round-headed owl, wood owl, rain owl, and le chat-huant du nord, which apparently is French for "the hooting cat of the North." That night, I carry Callie the mouse-catching cat just outside the door to listen, holding her close, recounting stories of a mythic past and ancient forbearers.

And once I have learned all this, it stops coming.

Wherein I rescue the latest mouse

WHY I EVER BELIEVED this was over for a while is beyond me.

Earlier this evening, Callie caught another one. Headfirst. Off she goes, slinking under one chair and then another, growling, scurrying off whenever I get near. Cursing, I chase her into the woodstove room and grab the scruff of her neck, thinking that if she clamps down hard, at least the death will be swift. I grab and shake; I yell; I consider whether I want to stick my fingers in between her teeth to try to pry open her jaw—thereby giving myself more injuries—and give the mouse a chance to get away. But that mouse is about halfway into her mouth, which puts its mouth about where my fingers would go. I don't trust the mouse to know I intend to be its savior. I shake Callie some more. No luck.

I call my sister. I am not going to endure this alone again, stand here helpless while carnage happens. Five-year-old Zoe gets on the phone and is philosophical: "Cats are like that, you know." My sister laughs and proceeds to offer suggestions, all of which would work if I had another human being around. Aggie is no help—she's too aware of how formidable Callie is. So I talk on the phone and chase Callie around. She's got it by the leg, she's got it by the tail, she's got it by the head again. She lets it go until it moves and then captures it again. I try to get near her when this happens but she is like lightning and never lets it go unless she's under a chair or near cover—some place I cannot get to. This goes on for about fifteen minutes, back and forth, from the fireplace room to the woodstove room.

Finally she drops it under the rocker; it scurries between the brick wall and a cardboard box. I grab Callie and throw her in the bathroom, then go back for the mouse, which is of course gone. This is one injured mouse, but I finally find it under Aggie's bed, and armed with an empty yogurt container, I trap it, scoop it up, and take it out across the road to some brush by the river. Will it freeze to death? It's minus five out tonight. Will the night predators get it? The owl? Who knows. It isn't in my house tonight. My sister thinks it'll be back; I tell her I don't think so. If it's stupid enough to come out from behind the stove where Callie's parked herself, I think it's too stupid to find its way back here.

No sooner do I sit down and slow my breathing than she pounces on another one, but it gets away. I set up a live trap by the stove; though I know peanut butter is best, there's none in the house, so I use some Thai peanut noodle salad left over from my dinner. Tonight, I lock us all in the bedroom.

In which no good deed goes unpunished

I WENT OUT THIS morning with Aggie to get the mail. From a low of minus five last night, it had warmed to just zero. There, on my side of the road, over the ice hump, headed toward the house, was the frozen carcass of a mouse.

Something tells me that this is odd. Why would a mouse stop in its tracks out in the open to freeze to death?

Several possibilities come to mind:

(a) Something got it during the night, played with it, and dropped it willy-nilly out in the open.
(b) This is not "my" mouse.
(c) It is my mouse, was making its way "home," but had been so traumatized and injured by its earlier close call with Callie that it just couldn't go any farther, halted, gasped its last, and died out where I would be sure to see it and be followed by paroxysms of guilt.

It is the last, of course, that lingers as I make my way down the road.

A pleasant interlude

I WAS SURE IT was just an interlude. I was sure there was more to come.

I went to the hardware store looking for the kind of large, multi-mouse, live trap that I'd heard about. I already have one, mind you, but it's plastic, and since three years ago when I bought it for use in this very cabin, only three mice at most ever fit in there. I'd heard about one that's metal, makes a lot of noise, and catches a lot of mice. The pest control section at Lenoch and Cilek hardware store is vast, and there on the shelves were the extra-large multimouse live traps, along with the plain old regular-sized multimouse live traps, and also the plastic kind I already have, as well as all the other assorted torture devices for killing critters, which I looked away from very quickly.

And right there in front was also a very expensive electronic device, which I had seen advertised in New Age–type catalogs and which looks like a plug-in room deodorizer or an electronic doorbell. When you place it in an outlet, it supposedly creates a vibration through the wiring and walls of your house, sending all rodent-like critters packing. The packaging reassures consumers that it doesn't affect electronic devices such as televisions or VCRs, nor household pets, except hamsters and gerbils, of course. In small print, after I got it home, I also read that it will increase the level of rodent activity at first, so it should be used "in conjunction with glue traps for the first week or so."

So the electronic device (which may be a huge swindle) is plugged in. And the plastic multimouse trap is set, baited again with Thai peanut noodles. And again we will all crowd into the bedroom tonight and close the door.

In the morning, there is one lone mouse in the trap, which I take with Aggie on our walk at dawn, way, way, way up the road to the old stall where three years ago a miniature pony lived. There may still be enough grain to distract a small mouse from wandering back to the house.

The wisdom of cliché

"WELL, YOU KNOW, IT'S nature's way."

"That's what happens out in the country."

"You wanted to live close to nature—well, that's nature."

"Mice are dirty, disease-ridden creatures."

"It's simply a cat's nature."

"You are just trying to make a rodent—a pest—into some sentimentalized Disney toy!"

"But that's what cats are for."

Early on, I should have started keeping track of all the things people say when you tell them that you have mice in your house and do not want to be party to your cats' torture and slaughter of them. They proclaim and declaim almost immediately, proudly, as if they are the very first to have said such things. They speak even before you can explain that the point is (a) you do not want to *watch* it, even if you accept the fact of it; (b) you do not want to have to deal with the veterinarian bills for worms, parasites, and perforated intestines after your domesticated cats ingest the mice; and (c) you do not want those cats' tongues licking you awake or pushing their muzzles into your face in the morning.

Things have come to this

FOR DAYS, THERE WERE no mice.

Then one appeared in the little plastic trap: a box with a flap that invites them in, then shuts in a way so they can't get out, has air holes and room to move around. Aggie and I took it way down to the mailboxes again.

I was learning that I couldn't shut the bedroom door if I wanted to stay warm at night. So I put Callie in the dog crate, Aggie slept on the floor by my bed, Ollie was with me as usual, because he's too frail to get down once he's up on the bed. And sweet Emmy, I thought, she won't do anything.

At three in the morning, I was awakened. How was it that I knew what it was even before it pulled me out of sleep? A clearly recognizable sound: jaw open, voice muffled by something furry. A sound I know well from our home in Michigan, where every night after I've turned out the lights, Emmy picks up one of the stuffed toys and brings it into the bedroom begging to play. But we have not brought the toy stuffed animals to the cabin.

Thankfully, Emmy is a much more compliant cat than Callie. I caught her, and made her drop the mouse. This happened several more times, and each time, while the mouse scurried, Emmy scurried, I scurried, and eventually, the mouse got away. Emmy was sad. I shoved her into the crate with Callie.

Next night, 8:00 p.m., Callie caught one. Same routine as before, only this time I watched until it was dead, because I wanted to know what she does with the carcass. When she started crunching the bones, it was more than I could stand and I shut myself into the bedroom until she was done.

Next morning, there was another mouse in the trap. Aggie and I took it to the mailboxes, but instead of scurrying down the hole in the snow when I let it out, it scampered out into the road, toward the cabin.

I buy a bigger, less expensive (because it's on sale), electronic *and* ultrasonic device, plus an extension cord, so that I can position it correctly. And, it's come to this: I set traps. Killer traps.

For two days, there have been no mice.

In which pride goeth before a fall

"IT'S BEEN TWO WEEKS—THERE are no more mice." I knew as soon as I had said this to too many people, I'd be proven wrong.

Last night, Ollie, Aggie, and I were all snuggled warm under a blanket on the couch watching TV when I heard the sound. A quick, decisive, firm pounce. By the time I got up and turned around, there was Emmy in the middle of the kitchen floor. She had a mouse in her mouth but a look in her eyes like she was just as surprised by this as anyone else, and now that she'd got it, she didn't know what to do with it.

This time, I'm quick: I scoop her up, keep a firm grip on her, flip on the outside light, am out the front door, walking away from the house, and I pry open her jaw. The mouse runs free. I pray that it gets under snow cover before the owl notices.

Listening to the river

JANUARY. I STEP OUTSIDE with Aggie at ten at night. Sheepskin slippers or felt clogs—whatever I have on my feet crunches and squeaks on ice and snow. If it is clear, the sky is dark, the ground is light—a photographic negative. The trees are bare lines and angles. From the cabin door, or from the windows as I sit and write, or in the morning when I turn over and raise the shade next to my pillow, I can see across the river. The white ground softens and illumines everything. How can anyone be afraid to be outside at night in winter?

Flocks of Canada geese huddle along the bank on the other side of the river, honking. More like braying. Are they distressed because we came outside, or is it just general unease, fear of predators? Does something hunt them at night? I don't know what preys on them. Coyotes? Could there be wild dogs on that side of the river? Or the eagles that fall from tree to river in the early morning as Aggie walks beneath them, as if they suddenly remember the need to fish? Clearly, I know nothing about riparian ecologies or the habits of wildlife out here on the river.

Although I never stop wondering about them, I am comforted by the geese huddled there, everyone curling up against the cold, for the night, for the winter. Sometimes I'll be out at dusk right when they gather, flock after flock coming in to land on the river's edge, deep wing beats fanning the last air of daylight over my head. Five, six, seven Vs at a time. I wonder, is each V a flock? What's a V of geese called? Do all these Vs find separate cubbyholes on the river? Do they travel separately during the day and meet up again at night? Is there a hierarchy among them? How many actually crowd in against that bank every evening? And why that bank, that particular part of the river, on the inside far side of the bend?

February. I go out with Aggie before going to bed. Something bulky, a presence, drops from one of the trees near the door, passes silently to the river, over the river. Aggie stands in the middle of the path and looks back at me. I stand stock still, shoulders involuntarily hunched, still reacting to knowledge that something had been there, lurking, just above our heads. The snow has gone, ice remains. When I carry the mousetrap across the road and dump its contents, I often cannot see the mouse, a small dark fur ball against patches of dark ground. More often, I simply have to trust I'm not dumping it on my feet.

March. I listen for the geese but haven't heard them for a while. I haven't heard the owl either for a couple of weeks. Instead, when I go out with Aggie at ten, hands dug deep into jacket pockets, boots open, laces dragging, what I hear from across the river every night after the sun has gone down is something familiar but out of place. The geese's absence weighs on me. Snow too seems to be gone for good. The world is changing, warming, opening up, and I am the only one sad about it. Wells of loss follow me for days and weeks. Even after I allow myself to believe that what I hear are peepers, believe that there is some logic in their appearing so early, I still cannot shake the absence.

At the end of March, nights are still below freezing. How can the peepers survive? What is there for them to feed on? How can anyone desire such a thing as spring?

Much later, after I begin to realize I can search for answers to things that trouble me, I learn from a website on frogs that *Pseudacris crucifers* are "among the very first to call and breed in the spring, often starting while there is still snow on the ground and ice on the lakes." If they have plopped themselves in cracks or crevices in the earth, their already loud calls "can create an effective ventriloquism: the frog sound seems to come from somewhere other than where the frog actually is."

Even though these facts give me some answers, it seems to me good that I did not know this last one when I first heard the peepers. With so much uncertain, so much flying at me from the dark, not to have been able to trust my ears might have been just too much to bear.

April. Peepers every night. Now when I open the door and Aggie dashes out, I lose her in the darkness. In that moment of blindness, I look around and up. It's not just the darkness of night, moon or not. With no snow on the ground reflecting light up, and no snow on branches, longer days bring darker nights. I scent moisture rising from the ground, wisps of warmth.

May. The moon is crescent, the air cool. I stand on the gravel drive and face the river. Fireflies here on the river seem different, more green than yellow, slower to move, slower to blink. They're like some sort of high-tech outdoor equipment. On. Off. Move. On. Off. Or, on. Staying on. Staying on. OK, off. Are they really different or is it the weather, the severe winter, the temperature? Or is the difference just me, just in what I notice, how I notice, how I attune myself to what's here?

I listen to the peepers on the river, across the river. Day or night now, tree frogs appear climbing up the cabin windows, underbellies smooth and yellow, pressed flush to the glass. I can no longer see across the river. Foliage darkens the nightscape, carves bulk and shape along the drive, across the road, at my back, in my way. We are canopied over, overwhelmed, soaking up moisture. When we step outside, there are sometimes human voices skipping downriver from far away, another shore. There are sometimes a few notes of music, a crackle, a second's worth of sound. A motor on the river, passing in a murmur.

June. Summer's dense, heavy smells catch my attention over and over, unexpectedly, often dramatically—yarrow tonight, pine needles on damp earth, comfrey. Abundance, indulgence, days opened out, all the sounds from outside moving in the windows on one side of the main room and out the other, like the light, like the Virginia creeper vines that have made their way over, under the foundation, from one side to the other.

Stepping outside risks being scented, sought, zeroed in on, covered and bitten, silently and invisibly. Even at the very end of June, after the solstice, as the days slowly, slowly begin to shorten and cycle toward winter again, I miss the geese. As best I can, I look around. But the shapes around me are dark and high, and I can only barely make out a moving shadow that is Aggie coming back toward me from the road, ready to go in for the night. Even though she will push against my knees, after I turn and shift and reach again for the old cat, we are not curling up, huddling, drawing warmth from contact. We stretch out across the feather bed, gaps between limbs dissipating night's heat.

The windows stay open; night noises ride the hours in waves. While my reading light is still on, we hear deer crashing around through the brush. On past midnight, raccoon and possum and groundhogs move across the yard; Aggie and the cats follow them from one window to the next, hearing more than I can, seeing what I cannot.

There's always something at about three in the morning. But last night, it was such an eerie sound that it had me wide eyed, lying there without a clue, listening. It was coming from the river and seemed to move. The other morning as we came to the river's edge through the knee-high Queen Anne's lace and oxeye daisies, I heard what I could only call a bark as I saw a great blue heron flap its wings, flustered, across the river.

Once at three in the morning, I hear what I recognize as the sound a cow makes, but it isn't. No one I ask later that day can even guess what it might have been. More than once, I am awakened by a high-pitched scream, on and on, of what I finally acknowledge have to be hunted rabbits.

And then there is the night that I hear a chorus of barred owls—at least three of them, back and forth across the river—again and again, uninterrupted. By four, dawn has begun, and individual signatures are hard to sort out amid the racket.

Aggie barks at random hours through the night these days, but not at any of this. I don't know what she barks at. I've never been able to see or distinctly hear anything moving among the vegetation that hugs and borders the outside walls of the cabin. I've shone a flashlight. I've waited in the dark at one of the windows till my eyes adjusted. I've strained and listened. Only early in the spring when I first opened the windows did I get scared or nervous about who was out there, whether a hand would reach in one of the windows—the one at my head, the other to my right, just there at the level of the bed. At first, I would yell at Aggie to be quiet and close my eyes again. But then I told myself to pay attention. Now I lie awake every night, from about 3:00 a.m. on, trying to tell the life around me by the sounds on the river.

Bald eagles, again

IN EARLY MARCH, I head to the Raptor Project up at Lake Macbride. A dirt road winds through the woods for miles, past random group campsites, entrances to ski and hiking trails, but on this day, muddy roads force me to park my car and hike in a mile or so.

A short hike on one of the trails leads to the dozen or so small structures of slatted wood—dotting the woods like camp cabins—that house the permanent residents, and a hundred-foot flight cage for the ones that will get released back into the wild. You can come on your own, wander, visit, read. The birds are there, mostly silent and inactive. You're asked to be quiet, respectful of their fear, and to maintain some degree of proper fear yourself, keeping your face and fingers away from the wire mesh, because although all the birds have been incapacitated in one way or another, they nevertheless retain the ability to inflict damage on unguarded human skin.

The first cabins along the trail house the owls, as if in guarded welcome. In a glade on the side of a cliff on the lake's edge are several more. On the front of each, by its door, is a paper sign inside a hard plastic slipcase narrating facts about the bird, its name, its history. All these birds are unable to live in the wild and live here permanently. The story for most goes like this: wing injured, probably by high wire, had to be amputated. Or, found by the side of a road, shot; left wing too injured to be fixed, had to be amputated. Or, blind in right eye, unable to be returned to the wild.

No one else is around. I move slowly from cabin to cabin, following small paths that wind steeply downhill. At the very edge is the residence of a bald eagle, who can see my legs coming before I can see her. Just as my eyes find hers, she opens her mouth and lets out that thin screech I have only heard in flight. Several times she calls, ducking her head each time, in alarm it seems to me. I stay respectfully back, trying to take in how huge she is, how close I am, what she cannot ever do, which is fly off this cliff and soar over the lake. Just then something catches my eye and my ears, and I look up. I hear other birds, returning the call, I think, and then just as I'm wondering if that's my overly romantic or melodramatic imagination, I see two large eagles circling above the trees. They are circling in closer and closer, and as they move into the hill, they are closer and closer to the tops of the trees. To me. It cannot be, I think, but it feels as if this captive bird—her name is Spirit—has called them, and here they are, meaning to menace me back or away.

A couple of weeks later, I return to the Raptor Project for the release of a juvenile bald eagle who was injured and has recovered. The sky is cloudless but the winds are gusting to fifty-five miles an hour. I stand in another spot on the side of that cliff, a big, open treeless field, with dozens of other people, children, dogs. Everyone is wondering if the release will take place. I'm wondering if I will even be able to see. Finally, Jodeane, the director, arrives with two other women and a cardboard box that once held a TV. They speak to the crowd from the picnic shelter but the wind carries their words away from me. Others crowd around the box as one of the women finally bends over, gloves to her elbows, then straightens and walks toward me. When she passes not four feet away, the eagle's head bent over, a sob rises in my throat, suddenly, from nowhere, threatening to overtake me, until I manage to swallow it.

Children are exclaiming, clinging, talking all around me. There's no silence as there was on winter mornings on the river. There's no silence as there is when I see rather than hear an eagle drop out of a branch above and head down the road. There is no silence because the wind itself is chattering with midday. In the eagle's eye, I find the silence, so

I stay riveted there. When the volunteer sets the eagle down in the field and backs away, it takes off sideways and in a moment is up maybe twenty feet, then down in the brush off the side of the gravel parking area. No one can see it. A handful start walking toward the area to try, even though Jodeane has said to expect this, and that we shouldn't try to find it, that we should just wait. For this eagle, who hasn't been out in weather or under open sky for a year, it's hard to figure out how to catch winds this strong, she says. Ten, then fifteen minutes pass, and most people turn their attention to something else—conversations, running down the hill, chatting about nothing. I stand silent, unmoving, trying to sense it in the brush. Trying to understand that sometimes when I walk the road, there may be an eagle larger than my dog, sitting, just off to the side in the brush, waiting out the wind. Twenty minutes after its release, it rises up to a branch, hangs out for about five more minutes, then takes off, fighting the wind the entire time, diving and twisting like a kite. And is gone.

▲

I cannot explain what reached up from deep within me and grabbed at my throat when the eagle passed by. At the time, I would have said that the eagle, fierce in its grip on the woman's forearm and in the fiery depth of its black eyes, and the owl, its calling so close it had rattled the window, were the spirit of this place—the road, the cabin, the river. Signs that it was bonded to me, and that I belonged to it. Part of the healing balm that was tending my heart.

Seeing birds

BY THE MIDDLE OF March, I've been realizing the eagles are gone
from the river. And so is the owl. I don't want to believe it at first, but
the certainty has finally sunk in. It has turned everything into absence,
as I turn my gaze to the window from the writing table and as I walk
at dawn, a silence that calls as I sit reading at night.

Then today when Aggie and I head out for our dawn walk—the sky
light in the east but no red ball bleeding above the horizon yet—as I
stand at the outer door ready to push it open, I see starlings at the suet
feeder in the juniper, hanging above the woodpile underneath. Starlings are common, but it suddenly occurs to me to really notice them,
to try at the least to be grateful for them. We walk down the road past
the mailboxes, and I hear a woodpecker having at one of the many
dead trees along the road. I look up and see its outline, a big one. We
walk farther down the road, and the geese, who no longer bed down
on the river, honking all night, are flying in overhead. Canada geese, I
verify. Not so uncommon, although they still amaze me when I see
them as they're coming in to land on the river. They're at eye level
almost as soon as they pass over my head, no longer flapping, still in V
formation, bulky and graceful at once.

Back in the cabin, I feed the cats, eat breakfast, bathe, dress, tuck
everyone in for the day, and head out by 8:00 a.m. As I leave behind
the dust of the gravel road and speed up on the blacktop, there in the
middle of Izaak Walton Road is a male ring-necked pheasant, running headfirst into the corn stubble.

I reach campus and park, then walk along the river from the parking lot by Hancher Auditorium to the English-Philosophy Building, about a ten-minute walk. The mallards stay all winter on the river, but as I cross over the bridge, I begin to realize there's a very different--looking duck there, diving and staying under the water for long periods of time. All black, short white bill, longer feet, differently webbed: it's an American coot, I will learn later.

At 5:30 or so, I head home, and by the time I'm making the left turn onto Izaak Walton Road, the sun has fallen down close to the other horizon. I turn my head toward the bit of wooded glen at the edge of the marsh, catch a glimpse of a huge bird near the top of the spruces. I stop, back up till I'm directly opposite, roll down the window. I get enough time to really look at the ivory color and dark stripes of its breast before it turns and takes off farther into the woods, as if in slow motion, as if deliberately. As if to say, Here is all you need to know. Though I've never seen one before, the hawk's red tail is unmistakable.

Ever since, every day has been like this one. My longing for the geese, the eagles, and the owls never leaves me, but I realize today that there is yet more here on the river, more I've failed to notice or attend to. I start walking each morning with a purpose, searching. What else lives here? I buy a book and decide to keep track. Not, I tell myself, like those crazy birders who travel around the world trying to tick off long lists. Just a small black blank sketchbook. No obsession with facts and scientific nomenclature. Just a record of what I see. My experience with the barred owls and the peepers has already reminded me that the habits of curiosity pull me outside and deeper—outside myself, deeper into questions that lead farther off the road.

A reaction delayed

LAST NIGHT, I SLEPT lightly, because although it's only the first week in April, it's gotten hot and I still have the down comforter on the bed. At some point, I woke up and heard retching. OK, I thought, so one of those cats is bringing up a hair ball.

In the morning, I noticed on the carpet what looked to be much, much more than any hair ball I've ever seen. I thought it was a litter box accident. But no. And then I remembered—it was over two months ago that I was on the phone to the vet, after Callie had devoured every tiny bit of one of those mice, and he had told me that I might see some vomit or something expelled in the litter box. I had not seen anything.

When I bent down with paper towel in hand to clean up this mess, I looked closely, and there, meshed together and encased in slime, were clearly discernible parts of mice—hair and skin and cartilage and soft pink flesh, as fresh and colorful as any hunk of chicken at the meat counter. That glob of indigestible parts had been sitting in her intestines for over two months.

I didn't understand how the bits of mice could have remained so perfect and pink. I didn't understand why they wouldn't have been changed by the chemical reactions in a cat's stomach. I was thinking about these things in such detail because the terrified creature was not in front of me being killed. Was that it? Was that the key to why this so unnerved me? The fact of death or killing was not what caused the punch to my gut. It was a mouse alive, being caught, being hurt, *aware* it was being hurt.

Bird notes 1

I begin to pay attention

BECAUSE I HAVE SIX months to live here, to really sink in, with enough time to exhale, to be willing to turn around and look at myself—to let the pervasive sense of loss and sadness loosen its grip on my heart a bit—I begin to notice the things I take for granted and have ignored.

Mourning doves, cardinals, blue jays. Redwing blackbirds. Gold-finches, the state bird of Iowa. All kinds of other finches. Ducks, which might be mallards or wood ducks, blue-winged teal or green-winged teal, pintails or canvasbacks or mergansers. Grackles, starlings, chickadees. Sparrows could be tree or field, chipping or vesper or lark, white-throated or white-crowned, fox or song or swamp. And American robins.

At first, it seems ridiculous to look these up in a bird book, but R has several on her shelves. I had always thought of bird books as things that little old ladies with safari vests use, Miss Marple–like, as they tromp around the woods. And because I know what a robin looks like, it takes me a while to think of using the books. Range maps show that American robins appear all over North America, from Alaska to Mexico. I learn that *Turdus migratorius* is a thrush—*turdus* being Latin for "thrush"—and that they migrate "in flocks by day," according to the Golden field guide. Further digging tells me that *turdus* is at the root of the English word "sturdy," the etymology of which goes back to the Vulgar Latin *exturdire*, "to be giddy as a thrush." Mapping these connections leads to a sudden memory.

Over a period of time when I was young, perhaps eight or ten, I received for gifts several plastic model kits of birds. Inside the small, thin boxes were tan, hard plastic parts, printed instructions, and paints. You glued it together and painted according to a numbered guide. A robin, a blue jay, a cardinal, a painted bunting. The memory comes close up and in my flesh. I cannot recall who gave them to me or for what occasion, but in my hands I remember the size of the box, and the shape and hollow weight of each body I held, and turned, and painted sitting alone at our cramped kitchen table. Staring at the marked, molded lines of feathers, or the eyes and beak, long minutes or hours of intimate knowledge burned each identity on my eye and in my hand. I knew these birds. But I'd forgotten I knew them. Although there was no down or feather or warmth, no fibrillating heart or pulsing muscle, holding it—the firm grasp, the gentle brush work—nevertheless gave me a sense of the lightness of the life outside my suburban kitchen window.

And when it was finished, and glued in place on the painted branch or stump, set on a shelf and no longer in my palm, I knew it to be a poor substitute.

We walk the road

EARLY MORNING, I OPEN my eyes before moving my head, before the radio begins, the announcer detailing the weather. The old cat may sometimes be still curled tight, an orange-and-white fur ball settled into lumps of down comforter like snow-covered hills, the dog asleep on my feet. Sometimes I have time to reach over the comforter and raise the window shade. While Ollie stands, stretches his legs, squeezes his eyes open, begins to move his old joints, I scan what's outside my window: a smattering of ponderosa pines, brown-tipped needles open and airy, then the road, the riverbank, and across the river to the bare woods on the opposite side, the hill of Ryerson's Woods beyond, tipped with dawn's pink or an engorged moon, setting.

And then we're up in a tumble, pulling on clothes, working stiff muscles. Checking the horizon in order to be out the door before the sun breaks through.

In February, without leaves on the trees, it's easy to manage. The sun's rising lines up right through the cottage window in the kitchen. I still have time, can walk the road slowly, waiting for the pink, the long minutes of changing hues. Sometimes I'm already down the road and turning back before the first tipple of brilliance appears. By late May, the earth steadily inching toward solstice, if I wait till the on-the-hour news finishes, I've missed it. It's more of a race: 6:10, then 6:00, now ten minutes before 6:00, pressing me, get out, get out before it's up. As I come out of the bathroom, towel in hand, I can sense it. Filling the cat food bowl, turning between counter and sink and woodstove, stretching and unkinking neck, shoulders, sides, I know. I know, now, we have to get outside now, and I acknowledge an anxiousness that Aggie barely contains all through those long minutes of morning's ritual. Sometimes I see the point of brightness on the horizon through one of the windows, as I move from one end of the cabin to the door, breathless. Sometimes it's all I can do to tumble out the door just as the barest sliver of brilliance bleeds through.

And in June, it's almost hopeless. In June, there's a different impetus to be outside quickly, because by 6:45 the dump trucks are rumbling down Izaak Walton Road to the gate of the sand and gravel pits. If we waited until then, we'd have missed everything anyway.

But even on days when the mist hangs heavy on the river, when clouds obscure the sun all the way to the horizon, I find myself impelled out the door and down the road. Some days, the rain and wind persist, and Aggie looks back at me, ears and tail tucked away as soon as she steps outside the door. But almost all days, curiosity wins hands down, and we go.

I fall out the door and down the drive, turn onto the road, sight the river's bend back to town. The road heads away from the river for a straight piece, its life at my back, one of the rented houses on my right, an unmown fenced field to my left. It's from here that, one day at dawn, I see the owl glide down off a low branch, its rounded head and colors only a shadow, its flight a silent, slow heaviness. Ahead of me, from where I'm aimed by the road, sweeping to the left, I watch the sun make its reach toward solstice week to week. In February, it rises ahead of me through the eighty-foot sycamore, hitting me square in the eyes. By March, it's moved to the left a bit—fifteen degrees, maybe—not so much that I've really taken to noticing it, still blinding me on clear mornings. But in May, it's so far to my left that I'm missing it, sensing an absence even in its presence. Now it hits me square in the back as I turn the curve at the mailboxes, to the right, to the south, to parallel the river, entering a stretch of the road that is tunneled by trees and brush on both sides.

In June, I wear a cotton shirt, grab the binoculars and a bandanna to swat the mosquitoes. Down the long road, around the bend, away from the river, to the mailboxes, a red or pink or deep blood-orange glow to the sky, walking, waiting, until there, there, just a slice, an inch, and then the rush of rising up, like time-lapse photography of flowers opening, eggs hatching, seeds sprouting, stalks pushing up.

There are mornings that the sun rising spills like molten orange juice, thick and viscous, a globe you can look at easily, wanting to walk into it. On other days, the very first and tiniest rising sliver pierces, blinding and yellow.

And then there was the time that misty haze hung above the fields at dawn as I rounded the bend in the road, and a perfect, frightening red disk appeared suddenly between the trees, sudden color amid fog and dawn. Fog hung over the fields and the trees, but the sky above was clear. I knew it would burn off in a while. But there the red disk hung, and hung, and kept showing slices of itself through the trees as I went on along the road away from it. Even when I came out by the large, old silver maple where the owl had nested, it was climbing but still red, still heavily filtered by suspended moisture, adding no light, no color at all to the world still hung in mist.

▲

I head down the road to find out what's happened in my neck of the woods. What's changed. What's gone on overnight. Who's been out and about.

There is a life in these woods, that brush, that riverbank, that marsh, which I do not have access to or get to see. In early morning, preferably at dawn or just at sunrise, I may find its leavings, its traceries, evidence of its presence, perhaps even a glimpse as it retreats from dawn into day.

I step out the door. A lilac hedgerow leads us down the drive toward the river, the dog and I, then we turn and follow the river. Past the pony shed and mailboxes, taking the curve to the right, we enter the tunnel of trees. It's here that dogs from some other house may start barking or come through a wire fence and greet us. It's here that I saw the line of blood droplets, deep red on gravel dust, leading like a trail into the woods. It's here I saw the crows mob the owl, the owl rise up, turn, and stare directly into my face. It's here the mosquitoes are heavy and the honeysuckle and wild rose are heavy, and the limbs are heavy with dust when there's been no rain, or heavy with rain droplets even when it has stopped raining. Saplings arch over, grasses and vines grow close. Any breeze passes overhead. There's a certain quiet along this part of the road. I keep moving.

Where the tunnel opens up, I can see to the river again as it comes through the oxbow. We pass a charred, hollowed stump of a tree that looks, through the grass, like a black bear, arms extended for embrace. We pass a huge, old silver maple near the ghostly foundation of a cabin demolished by the federal buyout after the derecho. Overgrown grass marks what was the drive, the yard, the doghouse. The maple's spread is wide, balanced, a perfect perch from which to hunt on the edge of the wide and empty field. Here two dogs live and roam free, and here Aggie will venture far off the road to scent their markings. Some mornings the Irish Setter is out and bounds to meet us. We reach the end of Camino del Rio and the beginning of the paved straight line of Izaak Walton Road. The white pipe gate entrance to the gravel pit is sometimes already open, but often we reach here just as the one-legged man in his new white pickup reaches the gate, hops out to unlock it, then drives on through.

At this point the river has bent back toward town, away from the road. At this point the sun is above the tree line, and the woods are behind us. Ahead of us is the road lined by ditches, the stands of willows between two plowed fields, the marsh in between. To this point only we walked in January and February, through part of March.

It's only after I start paying attention to the birds that we take to continuing our walk beyond this point, onto the hard-top of Izaak Walton Road. We step up from the gravel to a smooth surface and amble the straight line from there to its head at the rise of the railroad tracks. A wide ditch and thick shrubs line the road. On one side are football fields of corn, marked off and separated by windbreaks of tall, thin trees. We pass along the front of the Izaak Walton League; sometimes we turn into its long, gravelly, forsythia-lined drive. We follow it back to a grove of enormous sycamore and oak, in sight of the river again.

By April, we are regularly going farther along Izaak Walton Road. Past another drive, blocked by a pole gate and marked by the large weatherworn red sign for the Johnson County Quarry and Johnson County Auto Recycling. Past the quarry itself, a pond-sized hole in the ground edged by wide swaths of bare dirt and another sign—Danger: Unsafe Water Banks Ice. Here I sometimes hop the gate; Aggie wiggles underneath, following a dizzying map of smells. If I head for the edge, for a glimpse down into the water, sometimes I find one or two Canada geese or mallards hanging out.

Beyond the quarry, the ditch on both sides of the road gets wider and deeper, filled with water. Beyond the ditch, as far as I can see, a mix of scrappy underbrush, saplings, tough shrubs. A lone large, dead tree, its forks worn smooth, shed of twigs and bark and anything wind borne. We walk the road followed by redwing blackbirds, plopping from power line to dried stalk and back again, calling. Even in the cold of March they are there, but by June their *kreeees* are the loudest sound on the road. And then we are to the marsh, the water dark and still, winding back away from the road, on the one side among hills and woods toward the river, on the other side quickly entering a cool arch of trees. If we are lucky, the sun hasn't yet broached the horizon, but its coming tints the hilltop of Ryerson's Woods, the tips of trees and the sand and gravel mounds, and we turn back.

Bird notes 2

By the book

IT TAKES ME A long time to identify the bird nesting in the cedar right outside the cabin door. It bobs and hops around among the eye-height branches, the woodpile, then down to the ground to retrieve bugs or worms. It's there at eye level scolding me as I leave and return, a buzzing that sounds like a rattlesnake. At times it carries something white out of the birdhouse. True to form, I turn to books. I keep looking at the photos in R's field guides, can't decide if it's a winter or a house wren, try to follow the advice in the guides and methodically go through the identifying body parts: buff underside, not speckled; doesn't often hold its tail up. Finally, I decide it's a house wren. It's so willing to let me close, so clearly interacting with me. That such a small, chattery thing should be called *Troglodytes aedon*—a name for a prehistoric cave dweller—makes me start paying closer attention to the classifying names too.

Another thing I learn from the field guides: you can tell if the large bird spiraling high over fields and woods and roadsides is a turkey vulture if it holds its wings in a slight V as it soars and circles. Wings leveled straight across means it's an eagle or a hawk. I learn that a turkey vulture's wingspan is five and a half feet, and I learn to identify its silver flight feathers, like a ghostly shadow along its span.

One day in April, after Aggie and I return from our morning walk up the road, I am wandering around the side of the cabin through dew-soaked grass, surveying daffodils and crocuses and clusters of other shoots unfamiliar to me, when a flock of something sweeps overhead toward the river. My head ducks into my shoulders, as if I might be struck. It passes like a squadron of fighter planes in V formation: dark, silent, low, ominous. These are not geese, of that I'm certain, but I don't have a clue what they might be. I stare after them, trying to re-view details, to catch what it was that my eyes registered as *not* geese-like. For several days the same: in unexpected moments they come in over my head in silence, in groups of three or five or more. Finally I think to look in *The Sibley Guide to Birds*, the new Audubon Society bird guide that Jan at Prairie Lights Books had persuaded me to buy back in February when I was searching for the owl. It had been generating a lot of talk in the bird-book world, she told me, but I didn't care about that, nor did I care that it's as large as a textbook and as heavy, which makes it too bulky for birders to carry around while out in a field. Unlike the others, this book is a work of art, its page layout clear and spacious. Still, nothing in the individual drawings helps me decide on any specific bird. I keep flipping pages, randomly skimming details. Only when I read in the entry for double-crested cormorants that they fly in Vs like geese and are silent away from their nests do I have an inkling that that's what they must have been. There are, apparently, several types of cormorants, but according to the range maps, the double-crested is the only one that shows up anywhere near Iowa.

I'm on Riverside Drive heading into town on Easter Sunday; the road is quiet and empty. I'm stopped at the intersection with Benton Street when I notice a flock of birds, high, high, so high I have no idea what made me even notice them. It's a large flock and they are circling. I have learned enough to be able to tell that they're not vultures, but I can't imagine what is large enough that I can see them from that distance. I'm craning my neck and trying to drive, trying to see anything identifiable; all I know is they're white. A few days later, midmorning, standing by the gravel pit, again I see birds circling so high overhead I wonder how I'm able to see them at all. They disappear, then reappear, sparkles caught by the sun. I grab binoculars and am finally able to see: white body, black wing tips, long orange bill—they're American white pelicans. I have a hard time believing this at first. I know pelicans only as ocean birds.

Later I learn from the field guides that it's the brown pelicans that are found on the ocean, that the white and brown hunt for fish in very different ways. The white pelican is huge—twice the weight of a brown, with a wingspan of 108 inches. I have to think about this for a bit, then look more in the guide to compare it to the bald eagle's wingspan of 80 inches, then look up the California condor's 109 inches. I learn that they winter in the Gulf of Mexico, migrate north through the Midwest. A man I know tells me that he once worked in a church in western Iowa that faced Storm Lake, that behind the altar was all window, floor to soaring ceiling, and that through the windows every year in early April he would see them land in the lake, covering it. They would stay for a week or two, and then be gone.

▲

Late May and it's cold. Standing on the road, watching the river, I realize there's something different swooping and sailing. Swallowlike. It won't keep still. If it moves so fast and doesn't land, how can I identify it, especially when there's at least two other kinds of birds mixing it up over the river? I develop my skills with the binoculars, following an individual, focusing on key body parts—bill, wing tips, top of the head, underside. Finally I find it: a black tern. I'm still relying on books for so many of the birds I see because I've never seen them before.

Bird notes 3

The body knows before knowing remembers

IT FEELS LIKE THE slow-motion double take in a film. I casually glance to the left, at the river, as I drive in at five in the evening. Though I can point to nothing, I know I have seen something. It's uncanny how I can tell. I park, grab the binoculars, pick my way through the grasses to the edge of the river, and sit on a log near the rusted-out trailer for about twenty minutes, staring across to the other side, trying to distinguish dead tree and branches from eye stripe, talons, skewered prey. The first day, the bird takes off in the opposite direction into the woods, so I can't really see its flight. But I have a sense it's huge. For three or four days more, I see it on the tree, eating. Jodeane at the Macbride Raptor Project tells me the Iowa Department of Natural Resources (DNR) has been trying for three or so years to reintroduce ospreys to the area, that there are only a few breeding pairs that she knows of either at the reservoir or along the Iowa or Cedar Rivers. Later I consult *The Sibley Guide*, which tells me the osprey has a five-foot wingspan and "feeds on fish it captures by hovering, then plunging feet-first into water." I sit each evening, immobile, waiting to see this, but I never do.

▲

What instinct or subconsciously tagged glimpse told me early to raise the binoculars on a seemingly innocuous bird on a branch this morning as we walked? Blue back and wings, white underside, dirty orange at chest and throat. Then it was gone. But later when I am back in the cabin, reading over breakfast, I confirm in *Sibley*: an eastern bluebird.

▲

Aggie and I walk down past the owl tree, past the quarry, to the beaver dam, then turn back. On the pile of rocks and broken asphalt, something catches my attention, dramatic and orange. It doesn't stay long, but long enough for me to see an all-black head, white bars on the wings, and orange back. I have been reading in May Sarton's journal *Plant Dreaming Deep* how an oriole welcomed her to the house in Nelson, New Hampshire; I had assumed she meant Baltimore oriole. Now, checking my eye's memory with the drawings and words in *Sibley*, I learn that there are many different kinds of orioles.

▲

At the quarry, behind the chain fence, among chunks of rock and debris, scooting along the ground like the sandpipers I chased growing up on the beaches of Long Island, the song of the killdeer imprints itself on me. When we get too close, it takes flight on what look like swallow wings. Black cap, white at the eyes, two or three more black stripes along the eyes, white body. It feigns an injured wing to get anyone away from the nest. In June, I see them every day in the cornfield at the head of Izaak Walton, and I hear them everywhere. Its swooping flight, its plaintive *krreeee*—this is one of the first and one of the few that I can recognize by its call alone.

▲

I am sitting on the couch talking on the phone to my mother late in the afternoon of Mother's Day. Out the front window I see blue—very dark blue. I ask her, "What bird is all blue?" She doesn't know. It's not the sky-washed blue of a bluebird, and it clearly isn't the shape or size of a blue jay. I had thought birds of such a color existed in rain forests, not among prairies and cornfields. I wonder if I have imagined it.

A couple of days later, walking down the road with Aggie toward the owl tree, I see it. And I have binoculars. Even with lenses mediating my view, the fact of it continues to awe me. All of it, except for some bars on the wings, unmistakably blue. I try to catch its call—chatty, long, light, and beckoning—in memory. By the beginning of June, I am seeing a lone male every morning flitting down the road ahead of me, always ahead of me, from wire to branch, always along the roadside, always in sight. And finally I have learned to identify its song without seeing it at all.

Driving down the road toward the cabin, almost to the curve. A gray day, lousy for my mood but perfect for the colors. About a hundred feet ahead of me, a small bird sets down in the middle of the road. I know it. I say aloud, because the sound of it takes so many syllables and is so pleasing in its meter, "indigo bunting." I slow, slow, come to a stop about ten feet from it. It has not moved, almost fearless but not quite. After a few seconds, it flies to a piece of roadside thicket, then to another, and another, deeper and farther out of my sight.

But while it is in the road, and on the edge of the thicket, I know it and am held by the fact of it: lapis lazuli, deep cerulean, stained-glass-window blue.

▲

Just as I turn from the cabin's drive to walk down the road one afternoon, I see something across the river—something larger, different. So often now, my eye knows before my mind understands. What catches my eye and registers is something very long and curved. A beak, I think, but then finding my sight in the binoculars, I see that it's a fish. A belted kingfisher perches on a log over the river and eats. An hour later when we come back from our walk, it's still there. I sit watching for about twenty minutes as it stands still or flies from one log to another. There's no diving, but I can see the distinctive and very prominent kingfisher crest. Two days later, I see one perched on the electric wire above the beaver dam, stubby and bigheaded. When the dump truck comes by, it takes off. As we round the road back at the cabin, two are sitting across the river again. They look a bit like woodpeckers from far away, but now I pick them out easily, even across the river, my eye leading, knowing I've seen it before my mind registers the name.

▲

Early one Saturday morning, chilly but clear, walking up the road, I hear a distinct call but can't find the bird. Scanning the line of dead trees between the road and the Izaak Walton League's lawn, at the very top of one, I find it. It looks around, then drums, evenly, steadily. I make note of its features: ladder-backed, with a red head and cap, and a tan face. After that, I see the red-bellied woodpecker everywhere, learn to tell the difference between its drum and that of other woodpeckers. It takes me longer to remember that the name doesn't match what it looks like, to me, at least. It's not the name that matters, at this point. My eye knows I've seen something, something to stop and bring into focus, before my mind kicks in to try to recall the name or what any book has told me about it. I am walking the road and learning to pay attention with my senses, my instinct, a felt knowing. I am starting to breathe with this place where I live.

▲

Several times this winter and spring, I think I catch sight of a pointy head. I cannot be sure. But then one morning there's no mistake or doubt: a pileated woodpecker flies from one tree on the road, over across the road, to another tree, and stays there long enough for me to focus and see: exactly like the cartoons I remember from childhood. I

wait no more than a moment, though, after it rounds to the other side
of the trunk, to hear its drumming.

▲

Driving up onto Izaak Walton Road, by the last house I see a large
bird with a flash of white and realize it's something I've never seen
before. A redheaded woodpecker alights on the end of the fence—eye
level, back to me, very still, but looking over its shoulder at me, clear as
can be. Its white body in flight, its full red head and neck unmistakable, not the partial red head of the red-bellied woodpecker. The
whirrrrrr of its calling louder than the hollow of its drumming.

▲

And I keep wondering how it is that I have seen—so easily, so many—
birds that seem rare to me. Birds I'd not seen in any of the places I've
lived—not the beaches and hills and suburbs of Long Island nor the
pine-covered White Mountains in New Hampshire, nor the dry
Sierra Nevada. Neither in Michigan nor even here in Iowa when I
lived in town. All of them right here, outside this cabin door.

City girl

I NO LONGER CALL myself a city girl.

Really, I never did, as a rule. Only when I came to be speaking to people who were not city born and bred did I use the label "city girl" to efficiently explain why I am comfortable and skilled at negotiating the speed and chaos—some would say rudeness—of urban landscapes.

"I'm a city boy," my neighbor says as he's out mowing his lawn, trying to be cheerful about it, although he makes it very clear he resents whatever work needs to be done out of doors other than turning meat on a grill. When he says "city boy," he means he's from Detroit. He lives in the house next door to mine in Lansing, state capital, with a metropolitan area population of roughly half a million. When he says this, I think, yes, these lawns and houses and streets are like the Long Island suburb where I grew up, and his Detroit is like New York City, although not as big, not as crowded.

He says this because he sees me out on my hands and knees weeding, digging, transplanting in the many flower beds winding around my house. Each year, I try to eliminate as much grass as I can. I dig up sod, set down root balls of one thing or another. But the grass is persistent and comes back up between the things I want, along with lots of other things I don't want, even though I don't always know what they are. My neighbor sees me as a country girl. And I am, truth be told, happy to be seen in that way. Unlike my neighbor, I think of Lansing as neither here nor there—too small to be a city, set beside Detroit or New York or Chicago, but too big for the way I prefer to live. I hear traffic all the time. There is too little room between my neighbors and me. There are too many multilane arteries used by too many screaming ambulances between our neighborhood and downtown, too much suburban push away from the town's center. Downtown is empty anyway. The state workers fill it during the weekdays, leave it an echoing shell the rest of the time.

I find myself saying I'm a city girl when I have to explain why choked highways and bridges and drivers cutting one another off do not unnerve me when I'm driving, or why finding my way through subway systems and past panhandlers does not fluster me. Or why falling asleep to the ceaseless taxi beeping and truck traffic on city streets is a rhythm I remember and fall into pretty quickly. Although these are the things I prefer not to live with, there's a familiarity in my wiring, lodged deep in body memory.

But I do not know what to call myself when I'm yearning for the sounds of spring peepers and silence to fall asleep to, or of predawn heron honking and bird chatter to awaken to. Though I spent twenty years living under one of the approach paths for LaGuardia Airport in New York, yesterday I actually found myself startled by the completely unexpected and unusual sound of a jet plane flying low overhead.

If I reach back far enough, though, I can call up in memory what it was like on that dead-end street of my childhood, when there were potato farms down the road, a vegetable stand on its edge, and woods at the end of our block. Even after the woods were cleared for a new elementary school, you could cross the street that gave the school its name and climb a small embankment to get to still more woods and endless wild blueberry bushes. You could take a narrow sandy path back to what must have been the far side of the potato farm, although I never went that far into the woods. I don't know why. In my memory, I stand on the path still in sight of the school, people I knew, and paved streets.

This may make me sound timid about wilderness, but I wasn't. I was drawn to it and braver about it than anyone else I knew. I wanted to live in the wild, ran to the wild whenever I could. The other side of the school was marked out into playing fields, but in the far corners, beyond the outfield and goal posts, I constructed elaborate caves and settlements in the bits of woods left. I planned ways to live in the trees permanently. On long drives in the family station wagon, I stared out the window and scripted in elaborate detail an adult life in a house deep in the woods—once, it was an underground home built into the side of a hill. I planned to give birth in the woods; I assumed I'd be caring for dozens of animals, wild and domesticated. I was always alone there. And safe.

Eventually, the potato farm was sold and the woods bulldozed for new developments—the ones you imagine when you hear the word "suburban," unlike the streets in my neighborhood, which had been short spurs off the main arteries built up right after World War II, close enough for a quick walk up to the drug store, soda fountain, and grocery store around the corner.

For holidays and birthdays, we drove "into the city," to the house where my grandmother lived and my father and his sister had grown up. My grandmother's sister and her husband lived upstairs. The street in Queens was lined with these kinds of houses: two stories, each floor a different living space, the rooms laid out end to end, a railroad apartment. In back was a dirt alley. Up the street almost to Woodside Avenue was the butcher's shop in the redbrick building on the corner, with a statue of a white rooster in the window, and right behind it we could see the stables where carriage horses had once been kept. We heard my grandmother talk about her girlhood, when this was outside the city limits. And how later, as young adults not yet married off, she and her brothers would sometimes persuade a friend with a carriage and horse to ride to what was then "out in the country," which meant the farms and woods that later disappeared to postwar housing developments.

As I blissfully moved through grade school, we would sometimes venture back behind the school, to the edge of the housing and paved streets, back where the woods had not yet been cleared. Quite a ways beyond those woods, we knew, was the Long Island Expressway. But right there, not five feet from a new road in a new housing development, was a narrow asphalt roadway. Trees densely canopied it, weeds grew out of its cracks. We never saw a car on it. We were told—someone repeated from someone else—that it was the old road that city dwellers used to get out to the elegant mansions on the North Shore when cars first came to be owned. That road spoke to me of the possibility of finding a secret path, access to an undisturbed, secluded place where I could live and listen and watch.

And at least once a year, we would go to visit my mother's two brothers, who lived in different towns on the western side of northern New Jersey. We always went for Thanksgiving, but I have early memories, too, of being there in summer, at my uncle Ted's place, which felt expansive outside and was never finished inside. Or at my uncle Sig's, which was on the side of a hill, with a scary-steep driveway, a house full of angles and corners, a tiny loft with my cousin's bed reached by climbing a ladder, and a high-ceilinged studio filled with my uncle's canvases in oil or pastels. A wide floor-to-ceiling window framed the hillside, the valley, and beyond. The whole house was heated by a woodstove in the studio, which smelled of seasoned woodsmoke—like a cabin, and like no place I ever encountered in the city.

Sometimes, walking out of the door here by the Iowa River, or in a particular stretch of the road, I will catch a scent of something green, something I cannot identify by name but is instantly recognizable to me as being from those hills in New Jersey.

I think about my persistent longing for this place off Izaak Walton Road when I am not here, and about my deep sense of finally belonging when I am here, as a recovery of this landscaped story of my past. Not only from my earliest experiences as a child exploring the corners and culverts, ditches and woods where I lived, but also from the stories I inherited of the places my family had lived. I can tell you that I grew up on Long Island in a suburb of New York City, that I spent a great deal of my childhood and adolescence in the city itself, wandering, visiting. And that most of my extended family had all lived there or in its suburbs. I can tell you that and you see one sort of thing. But I can also access a different landscape that vanished quickly, as quickly as I grew, like the science fiction or cartoon stories where the paths disappear and the picture changes to something dramatically different as soon as you turn your back.

Neighbors

WHEN I WENT TO live in the cabin on the river at the end of a dirt road, I informed my family and gave them the address and phone number. My mother, a hermit in her heart but a city girl in her upbringing and in her understanding of safety, immediately began to worry. "What do you mean, dirt road? What do you mean out in the country? How far is it? Can you walk? Will you be safe? Do you have neighbors?"

The irony of her questions limited my responses to eye rolling, snorting, and head tossing. Not a pretty picture, I readily admit. But consider this. Both of my parents grew up in multiple-family dwellings in the boroughs of New York City. For the first twenty-five years of their marriage, they lived in the close-in suburbs of Long Island, in houses crammed onto postage stamp–sized lots and so close to one another you could see into the rooms next door, close enough to the New York City line that as a teenager I had routinely walked to a strip mall in Queens. Then they moved to the woods of New Hampshire, and for thirty-five years, they lived in a house in the middle of the woods, on a hill at the edge of a farm along the Merrimack River. It's at the end of a road far from any town, two miles to the nearest convenience store, although that had been closed for over a year, and three and a half miles to the nearest store or public building.

The land on their road is divided into one-acre properties. When my parents moved, there was frequent conversation about the cultural differences between New England and New York. There was the accent, the style of furniture, the presence of whole industries concerned with "country living," the necessity of owning a chainsaw. The woods were dense enough that no curtains or blinds or window coverings of any kind were needed, not even in the bathroom, because no one would ever be near enough to see inside.

There was enough forest between the houses that my parents could be out in the garden, and although they might be able to see their next-door or across-the-road neighbors out around their own properties, it would be possible to completely avoid even nodding to one another. For my mother—whose resistance to neighborly intimacies on our short, dead-end street on Long Island was itself the topic of gossip—this arrangement seemed ideal. Living in the New Hampshire woods satisfied my mother's desire to keep to herself, but her sensibility about safety was still an urban dweller's. I had come of age with a different equation: safety to me meant keeping a protected space away from other people, well guarded and alert for intrusions. Only in the solitude of this cabin, this secluded gravel road, this unexpected and mostly hidden bend in the river, had I begun to feel what it might be like to live without the weight of that guard. Periodically, I would remind my parents of the fact that if something were to happen to them—were a burglar lying in wait, were one of them to break a leg, were a storm to take out the power or some other disaster keep them from being able to get into the car and drive down the winding, narrow roads to some necessary public service—they'd be stuck. No one could hear them or see them. No one was in the habit of looking. For all intents and purposes, they were out in the middle of nowhere.

"Just reassure me," my mother asked on the phone the day before I drove to Iowa, "how far is it from . . . from . . ."—she didn't even know how to visualize it—"from stores or people or some help?" A day or two after I arrived, I let the odometer show me that it is three miles from the cabin to the intersection of Highway 6 and Riverside Drive—where one might find what could be considered "help." A KFC, and a strip of storefronts that includes a Dollar General, Arby's, and the new high-ceilinged and upscale location of Fin & Feather, a local sporting goods store. My neighbors on either side were close enough—as close as the ones to the side and across the road from her own house. To use her own favored expression, my mother buttoned her lip after I told her all this.

What I did not tell her, later, was about the fire on Good Friday.

In early April, it had begun warming up. Car windows were rolled down often by midday. I had already ripped the plastic off the windows, pushed up the storms, and pulled down the screens. But it wasn't warm enough yet to believe that a last bit of cold wouldn't come before that magic frost-free date of May 6. It wasn't warm enough yet to sleep with the windows open. It was, however, mild enough to take a bug-free walk in the garden after dinner at Carl and Kate's. As dark descended and we headed inside, Kate asked, "Do you feel safe out there?" It was not the same kind of question as my mother's. There was none of the anxiety, just curiosity. I unconsciously heard these questions, and answered them, as if they were asking, Aren't you afraid of bears and wild animals? Aren't you worried about someone robbing your possessions, vandalizing your car, knocking you over the head and stealing all your money? Although I had been raised in the "safe" suburbs, I had found a bravado with which to protect myself. In truth, I didn't really know what safe felt like. And I would not admit, even to myself, that I felt anything but assured that I could take care of myself, so used to guarding myself, fending off threats, and unwilling to take on anyone else's anxiety. "I'm not at all worried," I replied out of habit.

I drove home, pulled into the drive, and went to bed. At some point in the middle of the night, I found myself groggily drifting awake, trying to make sense of what was disturbing me. Slowly I realized I was hearing a far-off voice, outside, debilitated, crying something. "Help me." It went on, every few seconds, and each time it seemed to come from different sides of the house. As I tried to make sense of it, I imagined some old boyfriend of some former tenant, drunk, calling into the windows. At about that moment, Aggie heard it too and started barking. "Shit," I thought, and sat up. I looked out the window behind my head, toward the drive and the front door, and saw high flames. "Shit," I said out loud, more pointedly. Some drunk, I thought, had set a fire in my woodpile, which was way too near the cabin and right under a large cedar. My heart racing, I grabbed my glasses, put on shoes and sweat shirt, thinking ahead to how I might escape from this lunatic, found the phone, and dialed 911.

Even I could hear the trembling in my voice as I talked to the dispatcher, walking from window to window, trying to find the voice that was still calling. With my glasses on, I could now see that the fire wasn't in my woodpile but at the next house. "There's a fire," I said, "but there's also a guy outside . . ." And then I realized that the guy was at my front door.

The dispatcher kept me on the line. "The trooper is at the intersection of Highway 6 and Gilbert. He'll be there in two minutes. Are you inside? Is he trying to get inside? Is that your dog barking? The fire department trucks are on the way. The trooper is turning down Izaak Walton Road. You should be able to see his lights now." And indeed I could see headlights winding their way through the woods along the gravel road. So I ventured to open the locked inner door, moved into the tiny entryway, and looked out the unlocked outer door. There was a figure lying on the ground. I yelled at him, "What is it? What's the matter? Are you hurt?" and he repeated what he'd been calling out all along, "Help me, please." I told him the police were on the way and wondered if standing there with no barrier between us was a smart or a foolish thing to do.

The police car pulled up, the officer got out, and as they talked, I realized the man on the ground was hurt. He said he had come home from a club, had sat in his car listening to music, and had fallen asleep smoking. He had come to when the windows exploded and the car had filled with smoke. He had crawled on his hands and knees over to this property, to my door. His voice was hoarse as he spoke and he asked for a drink of water. It passed between our hands lit by the fire still blazing high into the 3:00 a.m. night, his car parked dangerously close to his dwelling and to the propane tank on the other side.

The fire trucks arrived, medics helped my neighbor away, and I stood alone in my drive, hugging a sweater, staring over the lilac bushes at the firefighters dousing the black shell of a car. At some point, the landowner who lived at the head of the road had walked down, edged toward the fire trucks, and turned to look at me, but said nothing.

I stood for what seemed like a long time, a thin breeze finally nudging me back to bed, though it wasn't chilly. The trucks and fire personnel were still there, and some part of me wanted to see it through, but the adrenaline had ebbed and sleepiness was taking over. Saturday was warm and lovely, and when I awoke, I barely remembered or credited my memory of just a few hours before. Aggie and I tumbled out the door at sunrise. I stood in the road again, staring at the charred skeleton of the car as Aggie sniffed and wandered. What kept me standing and staring, both that morning and the night before, was imagining my neighbor on his hands and knees, injured, lungs filled with black smoke, crawling for help. The straight line from his car to my front door would be impossible to cover. There was dense brush, a battered fence of rusted chicken wire, stumps and briars and dog shit. If he had headed toward the road it wouldn't have been any better. The stones in the road and my drive were large, not finely ground stuff but pointed chunks over which I often stumbled as I walked each morning. A dirt road would have been kinder, even if it'd been mud. What it had taken for him to manage to crawl—injured, choking—in the dark took a good deal of imagining. I kept measuring what I saw in the daylight, and what it must have seemed at three in the morning, against the images and fears that had nudged me awake and sprung me from my bed. How I had stood quivering behind a locked door with a phone to my ear while this man had—for how long—been leaning up against it.

What if I'd not been home? The next house in the direction he'd been crawling was rented by a man who was in the middle of a long-term hospital stay. The next house after that was twice as far away. Though my neighbor's house was unmarked by the fire, it would not have taken much for flames to have reached it and then his propane tank, and for the resultant explosion to have touched off the brush between there and my woodpile, this cabin, this propane tank. I had a good enough imagination for that.

About a week later, there was a knock on the door. There was never a knock on the door, because by the time a car pulled into the drive, long before a person could get to the door, Aggie would be barking and I would have reached it. This time, it was not a car but a knock that sent Aggie twirling in agitation.

It was my neighbor. I did not recognize him, of course. He had come to apologize and to thank me. He held out a long white envelope as he explained that he didn't know what else to do but here was a gift certificate to the Hy-Vee grocery store. I drew back as if it were a live electrical wire. "No, no, I can't accept anything. No. No. I can't. I didn't do anything. Please," I kept repeating. We both stood there, the envelope between us, each needing the other's reassurance and pardon. All I could see in that envelope extended to me was my own hesitation at the door, my own fears, the belated and meager drink of water. Need had come to my door, and first and foremost I had been afraid. My fear had been the kind I believed possessed people who lock themselves into city apartments behind bolted doors. I had been afraid of what would come in. Now I understood that it was not only invasion one might fear but distance. Not people coming too close but not having them near enough. Not their intrusions but their absence.

I told him to give the envelope to a homeless shelter; by this we might both be redeemed or comforted. We did not speak again. But each time he passed in his friend's van or saw me as he mowed, we each raised a hand in greeting, neighbors.

The barred owl, again

AND THEN, JUST LIKE everything else I was learning, because I had not lived through a year's cycle that would teach me what to anticipate, just when I had settled my mind for sure that it was gone for good, just when I had stopped missing it, I saw the owl. It was the end of April and I was walking with Aggie along the road, passing the house that had been taken down, where all signs of its concrete block foundation and doghouse were gone. The field was now overgrown with grasses, a big, old silver maple in the middle of it. I saw something large drop down into the cover of those grasses. The grasses erased it but I knew it was there. When we came nearer, it rose up to the tree, then moved to one farther off, then another even farther as we came even with it and passed its landing spot. And as we moved away, it returned.

A couple of days later, at sunrise again, Aggie and I came to the silver maple. I couldn't keep myself from hoping to see it, believing it would be long gone, yet there it was hunched on a branch, its body facing the river but its head turned toward us. After a minute, it flew off to another limb. In the same tree, not to another tree, not downriver, not fleeing. Through the binoculars I now carried every morning, I could identify its markings, the vertical white bars on its chest that name it.

By mid-May, there was a routine. When I walked or drove off at six in the morning, I turned my head owllike to see, zeroing right in on one of two large low branches, and it was there. In late afternoon or at dinnertime, the sun lingering longer and longer, driving back down the road in the cloud of dust that inevitably kicked up behind the car, I turned again, and again it was there. I knew enough by now to recognize that this was not usual owl behavior. What it signified I didn't want to question too deeply. I was so grateful to have it mark my way.

At least that's the way I wanted to think of it. My conscious mind inhabits and moves in a cycle, between alternate poles of rest and inquiry. There are times I want to believe the story I have created, preferring it even as I know it to be a construction, know myself to be ignoring sense and probability. And then there are times it suddenly occurs to me to wonder, to ask about something that's been before my eyes all along. For a couple of weeks, I believed the owl came to the tree and stayed there for me, the way I'd half believed the eagle was a sign for me—I even toyed with believing it was beginning to recognize my car. Or beginning to accept us walking past its tree at sunrise. I suspected this could not be true, but given what information I had at that point, I was content to believe it could be.

▲

I have been making regular visits up to the Macbride Raptor Project. I park and hike back in on one of the trails, far from asphalt. The birds are mostly silent and inactive. I visit this place for its solitude. In the silence, I can stand in the presence of each bird for as long as I need. I try to avoid eye contact but it's hard.

Among the buildings is one for staff, where they keep and prepare food for the birds, but rarely is anyone there. One day in early May when I visit, one of the volunteers is working. She fills in and confirms what reading online, in field guides, and in bird books has taught me. Barred owls frequent big, old silver maples. February is mating time. Owlets occupy the nest in late March through late May. Then fledglings move out to the branches of the tree, often dropping to the ground below, testing balance, moving through air. The adult owl will bring food and dangle it from a branch, making the fledglings climb up the trunk to get it.

▲

By late May, I have been walking to the tree every morning to see who's there. I've gotten so that I can find the owl very quickly, even as its colors blend into the bark. One morning, I see two of them sitting on neighboring branches, close to the trunk. They sit and stare, two fluffy things without chest bars. No parents in sight. Standing as still as I can, I hear what the books call "the begging call," like *ksssshhhiiiiiiiip*, a kind of rising sound. The next morning, there's only one. For a few mornings, I see one or both, and then they're gone. Each time I pass the silver maple, I turn my head and scan, but it's always empty, and a small place in my chest once again sinks.

The marsh

I'M SQUATTING WITH AGGIE by the side of the road, waiting for the driver of a white sedan, then a large white pickup, to roar by, the sound, the speed so aggressively opposed to what I'm doing. We got out the door too late this morning. Too much is on the road that sends the deer into cover for the day, the woodpeckers undulating deep into the woods at the back of the fields.

For the first few months that I lived in the cabin, I didn't walk this far in the mornings. I didn't come up onto Izaak Walton Road. Where the dirt road ended seemed to be where a tunnel of safety ended too. The owls and the eagles lived back by the cabin, in the woods, on the river. Once you step up onto the concrete of Izaak Walton Road, you are opposite the entrance to S&G Materials, the sand and gravel pit. The woods thin out, the river is far to the right and has taken its turn back up toward town. Beyond, on the concrete road, there seems to be nothing.

I didn't know then what was hidden there. I didn't know then how much you could see by just standing still and listening. I didn't come this far, to the beaver dam and marsh, because I didn't know it was there. Even when I was told it was there, I came but I couldn't see it.

It was a Tuesday in early April, on a clear day with high clouds, warm and breezy. I wanted to take Aggie for a long walk, not sure where we'd go or how far. At the first house on the road, right there at the point I'd never walked beyond, where the Irish Setter usually bounded out to meet us and a short-haired mutt puppy too brave for its size ran circles around all of us, a woman was hanging laundry, a young child at her feet. She started talking to me even while she stood at her clothesline, too far back from the road for me to hear at first. She asked if I'd seen the beaver. She said that the landowner's son had seen it building a dam. She told me where to look. I walked past the Izaak Walton League, past the quarry, to the marsh, halfway to the head of Izaak Walton Road, but I didn't see it, didn't know what to look for.

Even when, weeks later, I did see it, I really didn't know what I was seeing. When I saw the dam, I thought that was all there was.

On Memorial Day weekend, as Aggie and I made our slow ramble down the road, a man jogged by with Baby the collie, one of the dogs that lived in the house by the mailboxes. I had never seen the people, only the two dogs, Baby, who was eager to play, and the nameless other, who was skittish and hung back. Way ahead of us on the cement, I saw the man stop and look over into the ditch. Then he continued running, turned back when he reached the railroad tracks at the head of Izaak Walton Road, and reached me just as I was getting to the marsh. He pointed, and said the beaver had just been there. He continued his run; I stood and stared.

If you were canoeing in the ditch, parallel to Izaak Walton Road, you'd follow the water and make a right-hand turn here. But immediately, you'd be stuck. Because also paralleling the road is a barbed wire fence strung on tree stump posts, almost entirely hidden, submerged in the marsh water. The water zigzags back to where the land seems to rise up wooded behind it. Far back from the road, you can see that the marsh turns right again and continues, but out of sight. On either side of this open water, where the vegetation starts up thickly, crowded with staghorn sumac, willows, and here and there the smooth, polished thrust of a long-dead tree, you can sense the water is just as deep, but you cannot see it.

I stood and stared. I don't know how I'd missed it. It blocked the ditch where it widened, just before the submerged barbed wire fence, just before it opened up into the big water of the marsh. There was the dam, huge and solid and new. I just couldn't figure how I'd failed to see it. But I still didn't know what I was seeing.

So it wasn't until the end of May that I started standing and watching and listening to the places along Izaak Walton Road. Even when you know the value of watching quietly, if you haven't a clue what you are likely to see, or do not know the meaning or significance of what you do see, then you miss a lot. I thought I would only see the dam. Each morning as I reached the marsh, I would turn and stand, still, watching. After I started doing this, I noticed stumps of willow, some with the top parts still lying next to them, amid the vetch and Queen Anne's lace in the ditch on the other side of the road. Or I'd find willow leaves littering the road in scraggly wet lines crossing it. Yet still I thought the signs were all I'd see.

Once or twice, when we had just stepped up onto the hard surface of Izaak Walton Road, I saw a large, low, quick-moving animal with a long tail cross the roadbed by the marsh. Aggie's nose was to the ground; she didn't raise her eyes enough to see that far. But when we got to that point, she stalked the concrete in frantic spirals. Wet footprints were still visible, even on mornings when the 6:00 a.m. sun was already bringing sweat beads to the back of my neck.

I was learning to see. One morning when we were close to the dam, Aggie charged a movement in the grasses. I hadn't been looking in that direction at that moment, so whatever it was, I didn't see it. When I caught up, she was headed down a slim path of mud and matted greenery into the water. And there was a beaver swimming away from us, down the winding waterway back into the places we couldn't go.

From then on, we'd get to the marsh—Aggie often racing there, charging that same spot, anticipating—and stand and watch. Usually I'd have to use a stern whisper to get her to settle down and be quiet. And then we'd wait, for the slightest ripple, maybe off to the very edge of the marsh, among a few grass stalks. Just the top of the head, two small ears, and eyes watching us. But sometimes we'd see nothing, and after a long time, I'd turn around to watch the marsh on the other side of the road. It, too, wound far back away from the road at a right angle.

On that side, there was less open water. It was more reedy, and the tall, broad-leaved trees that edged it arched over, a tunnel of cool.

One day, we saw the beaver disappear off the road toward its den. Aggie charged, anchored her feet, and kept barking. I saw nose and ears disappear into the den. Figuring it wouldn't come out, I turned to the other side of the road, and after a few minutes, there it was swimming away from the road's edge. A different beaver? Another den? I couldn't figure it out. It took another week of morning walks to realize that there was a tunnel, a concrete pipe constructed under the roadway, connecting what the road bisected, two halves of one marsh.

I had once seen the beaver dive without slapping, like an otter, quietly. Then one day we came in sight of the dam and the marsh just, it seems, as the beaver was swimming from open water toward the den, toward us. Wary, it turned and swam back across the width of the marsh, paralleling the road. Then turned and slapped its tail hard. I smiled involuntarily, a response completely inappropriate to what was required. I'd never seen a beaver actually do this. It headed toward us, turned, and slapped again. Back and forth, slapping and turning. It took several of these before the silly, stupid grin left my face and I realized that this was a behavior aimed clearly at me and my dog, trying to get us to move off. It wanted to get into its den and we were in the way. Finally I got tired of Aggie's bark, so I grabbed her collar and backed off a bit. And then it was gone.

Bird notes 4

If you ignore it, they will come

EVERY MORNING AS I come out the door, its eyes boring into my head from the opposite bank of the river, a great blue heron stands still as a stick. Given its name, you don't expect it to blend in so completely. The unmistakable lethal yellow beak, white face, black head stripe, gray neck, and orange thighs. But no blue. It's so large that it skews my perspective: next to it, the trees seem dwarfed. I've known this bird for a long time, seen it elsewhere, flying and standing, but this one is there every day, like it's taken up residence alongside me.

▲

Once again I am driving and I see something that I don't even realize I see. Something large and heavy and bright white flies from the deeper woods to the quarry across Izaak Walton Road. I grab Aggie and the binoculars, and walk back up the road. It takes maybe twenty minutes to get back there, and I don't have much hope of finding this particular bird in the marsh. As I turn to go back, after another twenty minutes of searching, it flies off from beyond the quarry, back over the road to the woods. Large and slow. I recognize a great egret, the curved neck, the lethal bill just like the heron's.

▲

A fog-draped morning, walking with Aggie toward the oak grove to see if any of the owls who were chorusing last night might still be there. Through the fog, a wood duck flying from the river crosses the road, heads straight into the woods, and lands up in the trees. A few feet farther and I can see it, perched in perfect silhouette on top of a ten-foot-tall tree stump. In silhouette, the crest is distinctive; perched that high, on a bare pillar, it seems fake, planted, like a yard stake for a giant. The remnants of a ruined castle. Some hunter's joke. After a while, it flies back toward the river, heading away.

▲

Early morning again, walking to the quarry, through heavy mist and fog and the fast-rising sun. At the top of the completely dead tree in the marsh, two green herons perched, completely still. I have seen them fleetingly before, in flight, but did not know the name. I sat watching for a long time. So odd to see their chunky bodies at the top of the pale, barren stalk of a tree in the midst of the marsh, so different from the great blue heron—no elegant curve to the neck, a dark body and light-colored legs—but they share that very long and lethal bill.

▲

For several mornings, watching the beaver on the side of the road opposite the dam, I saw something swooping over the cornfield between the trees. I could never get enough of a clear look at a single individual. Finally one morning, as one slowly flew right by me, eye level, I could see a white band across the tail. I had to consult *Sibley* because I had never seen anything swallowlike close up, and then I learned there are different kinds of swallows, and this one was a barn swallow. The next day I saw two sitting on a stalk in the marsh, just hanging out and preening, picture perfect in the dawn light. And that evening, three or four lined up on the electrical wires overhead, silhouetted. This was a pattern I continued to wonder about: once I've seen a particular bird, noticed it, marked it, even read about it, it seems that thereafter, I see it over and over, often and easily.

▲

I had always thought of swallows as inhabiting cliffs and the eaves of barns, but as I read more, I learn that they are insect eaters, inhabiting marshes, ponds, and waterways.

I'm starting to expect that each day I will see something new, something I haven't a clue about, have never heard of. I had thought that seeing more and more birds, being surprised by what I saw each day, was simply a sign that I just hadn't been paying attention. I had thought I needed to learn to see, to learn the habit of looking, which is so easy to drop when other demands draw my gaze elsewhere. But now I wonder: Is it that paying attention has led me to see things that are otherwise hidden? Or is it instead, perhaps, that I have been paying more attention because I am surrounded by a variety of species in numbers that are actually unusual?

Only then does it occur to me that this place—this marsh, this river bend, this broken, wooded, neglected tract of land—has somehow managed conditions just right for the gathering of these crowds.

And only years later—after the marsh has dried up and the quarry has filled in—do I realize that conditions during this particular spring combined to attract and support this number and diversity of species. That the particulars of climate, business choices, and zoning decisions had come together to provide an ecology—a home—for us all.

Rising thermals

LOSS ACCUMULATES. Intrusions, invasions, violations, betrayals, a failure of heart, a failure of nerve, abandonment, neglect, humiliation, death. There's so much language for all of it.

After a while, language fails. Long ago, it had become simply a boundless longing, a cold and broken place.

But brokenness and loss is only one story. Listening to and learning to see the birds in this broken place taught me a different one.

▲

Midday and the moment in spring when the soil and rocks, the green surfaces and undersides, all take the sun and give it back. The air is without chill, the heart of the sun is welcome warming.

I pull into the drive, get out of the car. I don't know what has stirred up some old wound or fear. I'm fine, I keep telling myself. I'm fine. There is nothing holding me, calling me, requiring anything from me. There is nothing my skin needs. The air light, soothing. There is nothing I need to do, nothing I need at all, in fact, nothing pulling my attention past the present moment.

There is no reason to move beyond here, now, every temporal condition sufficient just as it is. An atmospheric equilibrium, when air or water may pass easily back and forth, and a membrane is no longer a barrier. My long-held, well-tended self-protecting membrane thins, dissipates. I lean against the hood of my car, its warmth hastening the melting of this barrier that has for so long held me taut.

Feeling safe under the sky to open my rib cage. To breathe, to take up space, safely. And then tears start spilling, without effort, without words, without reason. I exhale into the wide spaces, out in the open between cabin, woods, garden, road, river, with nothing containing restraining pushing constricting.

And in that loosening, in that spilling, in the opening, it is as if an equation finishes, balances. Yes, there are old wounds I carry, but instead of curling in upon the pain, tightening protecting withdrawing, I follow it, expanding moving swelling into the space here, and it dissipates, rising with the heat. There is no one here, no intrusion, no fear, no long-ingrained impulse to withdraw, withhold, subdue. It is rising, my breath rises, I spread my arms, raise my gaze.

And there above me, of all the spots in the wide open sky, exactly above me, three red-tailed hawks are riding the swelling, rising thermals. They circle as the tears fall and the pain and loss continue to dissolve, taken up, the broken and the healed, on the rising air.

And they do not move on. It is as if they have targeted me and for a moment I am hunted, but it is not me, it is what is rising, the air, the swells, the spiraling and expelling of earth's heat, of which I am part.

And when, after I have looked down for a moment to recall who and where I am, I look up to rejoin them, they are gone. The sky is enormous and unclouded, there is no place to hide, no obstruction from horizon to horizon, but they are nowhere to be seen.

In the ditches

DITCHES RUN ON BOTH sides of Izaak Walton Road. They are deep enough and wide enough that I could not jump across them, would need more than one step down into them in order to make it to the other side. They are, I'm guessing, waist deep, but I'm not going to verify this. In early spring, the layers of dried growth hide what I'm sure is a life I don't want to surprise. By May, what's growing in them is high and dense enough that it's unclear what I'd be stepping into, whether it would be stable enough—if, that is, I'd simply sink down into some goop of rotting vegetation or toxic waste.

Aggie is certain there's life down there she wants to know. Maybe even to catch. She stands alert, runs along the edge, drawn again and again to whatever is rustling in there. Peering down. Darting her head inches this way, that, following sounds, many things we cannot see. Sometimes a small rabbit sits at the edge of the road, facing the ditch, waiting, or a small something else has already moved down into the tangle of growth. Sometimes at a distance we see deer clatter off the concrete down into the ditch, disappearing back into the mounds and culverts beyond. Periodically we come upon paths, the brush matted down, leading back between the willows. Sometimes there are only patches of brown grass packed by winter, new green growth circling them.

Each morning now as spring unfolds, I walk up to the head of Izaak Walton Road, where it rises to meet the highway, past the corn-field and stands of cattails on one side and on the other, the small grove where I saw the first red-tailed hawk. I watch the ditches on each side, like my neighbor back in Michigan who comes out each morning, coffee cup in hand, to survey her garden, to see what's up and what's new. Surveying first one side, then the other, zigzagging across the road, I monitor the melting, growing, intrusion, change.

Some sort of white flower reaching above its green, flat leaves—what I later learn is wood anemone.

Blue flag iris in the swampier parts, a lighter shade of purple, easy to miss unless you look closely.

Three huge bushes of wild roses, one marking the long drive back behind the quarry, two marking the fence posts at the head of Camino del Rio. Whether these are the multiflora rose, the invasive species, or something else lovely and benign, or the wild rose that's Iowa's state flower, I do not yet know.

Crown vetch, purple, white, or pink, like very large clover, growing in mats and lengths, edges and clumps.

Mullein, some still erect and dried from last year. Some beginning to thrust upward, to bulge, blossom heads ready to erupt.

Milkweed, the pods of which attract monarch caterpillars and will open up to floss later in the fall. Milk thistle. Grapevine. Bindweed. Queen Anne's lace. Oxeye daisies. Phlox.

Goldenrod—*Solidago*—native to this continent and not, it turns out, what causes hay fever. Its pollen is waxy and heavy, borne by insects not air. I read this in several places. I repeat it to several people, all of whom respond with some variation of "Oh yeah? Well when it blooms, I'm miserable." Which is what the books say: it blooms at the same time as ragweed but it's ragweed that causes the allergies. I don't know what ragweed looks like. The goldenrod is a tough plant that thrives in poor conditions. A perfect ditch dweller.

Daylilies of course, and lots of swamp willow saplings, lining the ditches. On one side, they spill up and beyond the ditch, a small grove or forest of willow. Only after weeks do I notice that many of them are only one foot high, gnawed to a pencil point. Then I understand the wet willow leaves sometimes trailing across the road in the mornings.

Spiderwort starts out in midspring looking like grass. Straight-up stalks with wide blades that trail like spider legs. Days later, little green bulbs bulge out on top. Then three-petaled stars of blinding, glowing purple open, dotted yellow in the middle. As I walk down the road scanning the ditches, these iridescent purple stars shine, so piercing you cannot help but turn to look again.

The wildlife inside

LADYBUGS, OR ASIAN LADY beetles, which crowd into the bathroom while February is dead cold, hanging out on the ceiling and the blue aluminum window blinds, falling into the bathwater and the toothbrush holder, crawling then flying across the ceiling, on their backs on the kitchen counter, feet waving the air. Their dried shells collecting in corners as March thaws.

Spiders. Huge ones with two-inch legs. Tiny ones, the size of the head of a pin, moving in fits and starts, like a computer cursor gone haywire. Very black ones—fiddleback, I think, although they move too fast for me to get a really good look at the yellow markings on the back segment. The ones the cats play with. The ones that bite me under the covers. Spiders in the bathtub every morning during May and June, scrambling up its turquoise enamel sides, sliding back down, scrambling away from the foam cup or empty plastic container I use to catch and transport them.

Wasps appear next, quietly buzzing at the screens or windows, sucking light, desperate. I take up the foam cup again, trap one or two at a time, slide a creamy sheet of paper between glass and cup rim, and carry them out the back screen door. They appear grateful when I shake the cup upside down.

And after that, ants. All over the kitchen. Very small ones. Too small to save. I get careless.

Flying ants—or some creatures that look like ants with wings— flitting around uncontrollably, now walking, now flying, drawn particularly to the breakfast table during May, caught up between the lampshade and the bulb, so even the cats can't get them. Collecting at the window's edge, or near the ceiling, always in swarms, unfathomably busy. Could they be mayflies? When I think the word "termite," I find myself looking the other way.

Ticks. They come in on Aggie in May, drop off, find their way into the green wool blanket still crumpled on the couch, still necessary some evenings. They appear in the morning on top of the bedcovers. Or find their way under my fingernail as I mindlessly scratch Aggie's ear.

Even a frog or two.

And mice. In January, February, March. June. December. Anytime. All the time.

In which I am taunted

HOW IS IT THAT I knew as soon as I opened the door to the cabin? What did I see? The deep rose–colored throw rug bunched up, as if Callie and Emmy had been roughhousing? Their too-eager greeting at the door, though it was only 3:30 in the afternoon, as if to say, Wait till you see what we've made for you! What did I intuit? Why did I know, even before I took a step inside or could see past the top of the wicker couch to the small gray corpse lying there in the middle of the beige Berber carpet? There it was, its fur matted with moisture (where did that come from? did they carry it around in their mouths all afternoon? did they sit there drooling on it, each preventing the other from snacking on it before I could get home?), its little mouth bloody, and very certainly dead.

I looked around at things like the blanket on the couch, also bunched up, and the seat of the chair where I sit at breakfast. Where has it been? Where has it been stalked and tossed and dragged about? Do I dare look at the bed?

Or is it that somehow they knew I had started packing the boxes at my office, and this was their way of saying, Look here, we've been doing this every day when you're gone to the office, but because *someone* keeps eating the evidence, you have been clueless. We just want you to know what we're going to miss when you take us away from here!

Then old sweet Ollie came out of the bathroom, where he sleeps all day in a basket under a heat lamp. "And were *you* part of this too?" But no, this corpse was news to him, because he suddenly noticed it with great interest, wanting to smell. After I covered it with a paper towel, I let Aggie out of her crate, which at night is known as kitty jail. She's so happy to see me, so anxious for the possibility of an early dinner, that she doesn't even smell it or notice it.

Callie the carnivore is curled up in her little self-made nest on the back of the couch right now, asleep, but has just made this coughing, snorting, wheezing noise in her throat, which makes me wonder how *many* of these corpses there were. Had one of them been midday snack, and another—a surprising surplus they could afford to leave for me to find?

I'm done speculating. But this better be the last corpse I find. There are still about ten days to go before we have to move back to Michigan.

I step outside in late June

I STEP OUTSIDE THE cabin door. I lift my feet, sockless now in worn blue Birkenstocks, the ones I slip on as my feet swing over the bedside. Cool dew coats my toes, darkens the leather.

I step outside as everything is reaching toward solstice, another day of cloudless sky, heat settling in, ready to open and bloom fully in a couple of hours. I walk to the back beyond the shed, to dump coffee grounds on the compost pile. I keep watch a few steps ahead for snakes. I watch not because I'm afraid of them but because that first glimpse with my foot in midair, about to come down on one, never fails to jolt me. Years ago when I lived in the little house in town, my lawn mower found and mangled and spit out a small garter right in front of me. What makes me cringe when I see a snake is the instant unbidden replay of that image. It's the harm we can so easily do unawares, without remedy, that haunts me.

I step outside and know myself. Know that I am right in my skin. That I am in the right place. This is what I tried to describe to friends and a real estate agent in Michigan when I said a house with a flat yard, where passing between house, door, and yard is fluid and visual. I look out the large back window, or the three front ones, and the green, the grass, the bleeding heart, iris, weigela are right there. Only eighteen inches between the floor and the window: visually, physically, I have full-body access to the outside. From my writing table I can see sweet peas creeping up to the doorstep as they bloom in succession on the stem, comfrey bending under the weight of bees visiting blooms of pendulous blue, dogs from beyond these woods nosing through the brush, turkey vultures circling over the back pasture. I stand and stretch from the keyboard, and in three steps I walk through the door. I am outside, brushing aside hostas and poppies that have pushed up from a crack in the stone doorstep, turning left, to the road or right, back to pump house or shed or compost pile. The wren is nesting not four feet from the door, the snakes are hanging out in the doghouse or the woodpile or the pile of bricks. I step outside, a world unfolds.

When days have been in the eighties and nights in the sixties, the moisture that has been gathering during the day settles and hangs heavily on the ground, on leaves and stalks and branches. Moisture settles and scent rises. Along the road, you can smell the mowed grass, the unmowed grass growing in five-foot-tall hedges. Every so often, you breathe in wild rose, breathe and know even before you turn your head to see it. Every so often you find small bunches of purple-flowered vetch. Waist-high walls of lovely, drooping, patterned poison ivy, *Rhus radicans*, lining whole stretches of the way. Virginia creeper reaches tendrils beyond the margins, into the road. Along the road, you are surrounded by patches of composed color and texture. Between the dense thickets of sandbar willows and burr oak saplings and walnut saplings and silver maple saplings, the wild rose and the eighty-foot sycamore, patches and clumps of still other tallgrasses, dark green at their base. Stopped in your tracks by swaths of red purple or the palest green, airy panicles set against the dried-blood red of last year's dock, you can see why the Impressionists were moved to use short, light dabs of careful color. Along the road, you are surprised to find the purple stars of spiderwort turning faces to you, the blue flag iris set neatly between panic grass, wild oats and brome, pepperweed, milkweed, and large spreads of white anemones.

On days like this, reaching toward solstice, in Iowa, along a river, moisture is slowly gathering, waiting for the next storm system to come through. Sun rises as mist still lies on the river, hangs in pockets, in slight depressions, settles over the marsh. Sun rises to a clear sky, but an hour or so later, the sky is white, faded from one pastel to another. Walking the road in the fullness of late June, you wonder how anyone can still be asleep, abed, about any business but attending to the fully wakened world.

I follow the indigo buntings down the road. I check in on the owl fledglings each morning and evening. I sit on the back deck, the gray catbird endlessly blithering in the thick wall of Scotch pine in back. I have come to know them too. I have come into an intimate knowledge of all these birds, a knowledge born not only of field guides but also of time, attention, care, and a place that provided the conditions for life and song. Two years later, conditions had changed, and they were not there.

In which I finally outsmart the cat

I SHOULD HAVE KNOWN. I should have known that if I said it was the last one, I'd be proven wrong. Again. I should have paid attention to that little voice that told me I was speaking wishfully yet again.

So I'm in the bedroom trying to clean Ollie's face because he can't groom himself very well anymore, but he's clawing my arm and making some unearthly sound. I'm feeling like a horror film villain torturing the aged and infirm. I hear a scramble in the other room. And I know, because well, it just has a different sound to it. I find Callie under the couch, Emmy stalking nearby.

But I've had it. I've just had it. I whip everyone else into the bedroom, lock it, and go in search of a very long-handled broom. I get a towel in one hand, the broom in the other, and open the front door—the one to the arctic entryway. I spend about ten minutes chasing Callie around, trying to get her into the entry. She gets under every single piece of furniture, but I'm on her, poking her, using the towel to keep her from rushing through my feet. Finally I get the towel on her head; she doesn't move, probably because it's too much for her pea-sized brain to simultaneously hold on to the mouse, zigzag away from the broom, and figure out how to see past the towel.

With the towel on her head, I pick up her and the mouse, carry them into the entry, close the door, secure my grip, and go outside. It's very dark. No moon. Only the lights from inside shining out through the windows. I hold her upside down over the flower bed and shake. I yell and shake. I blow in her face. I grab her two front paws and hold them away from her mouth—because throughout this, she's using them like hands to hold on to that mouse, which is probably already dead for all I know, but I don't care. I am bigger and smarter than this cat and will not be defeated.

I'm determined, but at this point I'm stuck—until I remember that there's a pot of water out back by the pump house. If only I can make my way through the grass in the dark and not step on or bump into any other critter. I get back there, secure my grip again, and dunk her head in the water. Voila. Boy, is she ever surprised and pissed. I mean, this is totally outside the realm of her experience. I don't know whether the mouse is dead or alive, and I'm not going back to find it. At least I'm not listening to a cat crunching on bones and sucking the hair out of her teeth.

If only I had figured this out earlier.

The last rescue

SITTING AT THE BREAKFAST table on the last day before I leave to return to Michigan, I finish my yogurt and put the bowl down for Emmy to lick. When I call her and she doesn't come, I'm not surprised—she tends to be cautious and to hang back.

But neither does Callie come, and that's surprising. I can hear the bell—the one I put around her neck to give the mice a microsecond head start—but she's not coming. So something must be up, and I go into the big room.

It's funny when cats have found something to amuse themselves, something that doesn't run very fast. They sit erect, watching, sticking out a paw every once in a while to change the course of the game. It's usually a large bug or spider. This time, it's a frog—about the size of a golf ball.

I cup it—easily done—and take it outside, only to discover that it's really only about half that size, because there's as much dog and cat hair matted on it as there is frog flesh. We go back by the pump house. I put it in the water bowl, trying to get the hair off, which is tangled and matted around its legs. When I'm done, it's slimy, shiny light green, a peeper I think, one of the ones that I now see, belly side toward me, on the windows every evening. No teeth marks. A clean rescue.

Leaving, again

IN SOLITUDE AND SILENCE here on the river, I'd found safety. I'd found solace. I'd found enough emotional space to unclench my heart. And in time I'd found joy. These were things I had not realized had been absent most of my life, had not known were possible, except in that small corner house in Plum Grove.

Much had unfolded, much had taken root. In the river's waters, in the tears to which I'd given a freer rein, I had been watered. I'd found myself looking more squarely in the face the depth of sorrow. Along this stretch of land off Izaak Walton Road, I'd found a rendering of the spiritual ecology—the psychic space—that I'd carried with me for so long. Paying attention to the birds had led me to being better able to attend to what was deeper inside and behind me. I had tapped into a well-protected core. It was a beginning.

I came to the river in a white time, an ice time, a barren time. Now as summer's solstice ripens, there is lushness creeping in at the windows—the trumpet vine that covers the antenna next to the back window is as tall as a tree, sending up shoots everywhere but mostly right up against the cabin, where they find purchase in the screens.

I walked down the road this morning, out past the beaver dam and marsh to the cornfield at the end of the road. I have learned to wait and watch for the beaver, and the deer, and the swallows and killdeer in the cornfield, to know that a possum lives out among the stubble, and that the marsh goes way back beyond merely where I can see. Learning to know this place has taken time and attention, a gradual unfolding.

When we had almost reached the railroad tracks today, where Izaak Walton Road meets old 128, I left the road, following Aggie down over the ditch into the cornfield, following the tractor treads. I turned around. I was about a foot lower than the road. A very loud motorcycle went by, sped out onto the main road. I turned and saw from a different angle, a different perspective. It had not occurred to me before to step off the road, step onto the path and down onto the field. All winter, then thawing, then spring, now summer, I have stepped gradually into new territory, new ways of seeing. Now yet another step, another move into the unfamiliar and the unfolding. From here, the road is a dangerous place. What's actually on Izaak Walton Road is, from this angle, an intrusion, sometimes deadly.

I will leave here tomorrow, the first day of summer. New ways of seeing have opened up to me. Perhaps I'll be back. Perhaps there will be something else. Perhaps, turning around even now, I'll see something in this place, this time, that I have not yet been able to see.

Season end

I CAME BACK TO Izaak Walton Road again for a couple of days that November, when the harvest had finished and the abundance that had so overwhelmed me in spring as it emerged had finished its season. R was in Belize, and I hadn't been able to get in touch with her to get permission to be in the cabin. I stayed with friends in town, but every morning at dawn, I drove down to the river with Aggie, parked in the cabin's drive, and walked as we'd been used to walking, up the road, past the houses where other dogs lived, to the marsh, past the beaver dam, up to the tractor access to the cornfield where the possum used to hang out and the deer crossed.

On the way, in the habit I'd taken up just a few months before, I spoke out loud: grackle, chickadee, cardinal, goldfinch, mourning dove, crow, ring-necked pheasant at the back of the marsh, sparrows, of course, hairy woodpecker. I knew how to spot them, where to look. I knew where the deer, hooves clacking across the pavement far up ahead of us, entered the brush and moved deeper into the groves of sumac.

But when we got to that point, I found the marsh was dry. The beaver dam was gone and so, it seemed, was the beaver. I stood staring for long minutes. The grasses held November's reds and russets in sweeping brushstrokes of color. Frost capped them at dawn, and by the time the sun topped the trees, it had turned to mist. The colors made the marsh the most beautiful I'd yet seen, but once again I was pulled by the absences. I had missed summer's ripening. I had missed a part of the cycle of life on the road, on the river.

There was nevertheless something new. Soft tan or gray, with a light underbelly, yellow fringe on its tail, and a crested head. A beak like a cardinal's, but pointier. Black eye band, black along the sides of the wings, dark under its tail. A young tree along the road, beyond the marsh, was full of them, maybe thirty or more. They didn't budge. Like ornaments. Like wax candles waiting for Christmas. Back in the car later, I had to consult *Sibley*, and I found they were cedar waxwings. Had I seen them last spring? If I had, I'd forgotten. I didn't recognize them.

When we got back to the cabin, Aggie was confused, couldn't understand my words: "No, I don't have a key. We can't go inside. We don't live here anymore."

It didn't make sense to either of us.

PART IV

EARTH ⋀ MARSH ⋀ SKIN

To those devoid of imagination, a blank place on the map is a useless waste;
to others, the most valuable part.

—ALDO LEOPOLD, *A Sand County Almanac*

Going home

HOW MANY PEOPLE HAVE told me, "You can never go home, you know. You can never go back." It is always said with a particular tone, a particular tilt of the head and turn of the mouth. As if I should have known this. As if something I have said has made the necessity of voicing this cliché slightly embarrassing—whether for me or for the speaker is not entirely clear—as if it should remain unspoken and unchallenged.

An old friend, who is fond of seamlessly tossing lines from early twentieth-century American novels into the business of his own and his friends' lives, sent a Christmas letter, from which I could not gauge his tone or intent: "I was pleased to hear that your Iowa venture went fairly well. Was it designed to be some kind of Gatsby-esque recapturing of the past? 'What do you mean you can't repeat the past, Nick?'"

▲

Two years later, another January. When I walked into the cabin last night, the car still packed and still running in the drive, I stopped short and spoke out loud. "Oh." A single word.

R had been back in the fall; she had moved the wicker couch back against the wall, the way it had been the first time I was here. It struck me as a rebuke, a firm slap on the wrist for having moved it. I debated leaving it there. I hesitated for just a moment, wondering if my concern with furniture arrangement was some kind of magical thinking, a belief that I needed to have everything exactly as it had been the first time I stayed here.

Some of the piles of books, the paintings on the walls, the large conch shells in the corner on the floor had been rearranged. The Desert Rose dinner dishes were in the hutch now, plants were arranged in the bathroom, and there was a large rust spot on the enamel kitchen sink where the faucet dripped. The water pressure was much reduced and I didn't know why. The halogen desk lamp that was on the kitchen table the first time I was here, and was broken last year, was now on the shelf beneath the pinned butterflies. I noticed the things I had left for R, some of them mine, some I'd bought for her—a toaster, a washcloth, small candles, a coco fiber mat outside the entryway, and a soft green blanket I'd bought at a yard sale. In these small ways, it felt as if I have been making the place mine. I began to wonder about offering to pay for improvements, like a new window or two to help insulate the front room better.

It took a couple of hours to clean up—to throw out the single mouse carcass and put the poison away, scrub the rust and clear spider webs. Plug in the refrigerator, make the bed, lay down the litter box for the cats. Throw a couple of rugs in front of the fireplace, bring in some wood.

Here on the river, I slide simply into these rhythms—keeping the woodstoves going, transferring food to mouseproof tins, taping plastic to the windows. It's not that it's easy to live in the cabin. It's just better. I walk, I listen, I pay attention. There's silence and solitude. By the time I went to bed under the down comforter, there seemed to have been no lapse in time at all. I was home.

▲

In the cabin, I sit at an old yellow-painted table to write. I sit between the windows facing the road and the river and the western sky in front, and in back the dawn, the pump house, the wooded fields, long, low windows, the ground outside close enough to touch. On this side of the river, jays, finches, cardinals, nuthatches, chickadees, downy, hairy, redheaded, and pileated woodpeckers, and mourning doves. Over the river, sea gulls and terns, and on the river, Canada geese. On the other side of the river, bald eagles and crows. Inside the cabin, Callie the calico climbs to the top of the heat ducts or refrigerator to survey the room, black Emmy searches out soft places to curl up, and Aggie moves from window to window, continually alert for all that is out there.

Many things have changed over the past two years. Ollie the old cat is dead. Kate Klaus is dead. My mother and father, my brother, and several close friends have all declined in health. It's no longer an option for me to secure a teaching appointment or move here permanently. Several friends have moved away.

Many things have changed, but nothing has changed about how I latch on and sink into this place. In this place, I unclench. Everything in me settles, and I am able to touch the deepest parts of myself, to keep company with the deep-dwelling sadness.

Many things have changed, but still there is the fire, the silence, the river, the dog's bounding down the road, and my own tender spirit.

Sitting in this room, with the fireplace dancing, the animals curled up in front of it, the windows along both sides extending my eye's reach out into the woods, the brush, the dirt road, the river and then across the river, I am safe, I am home. At dusk, flocks and flocks of Canada geese come in to land on the river, huddled in the curl of its elbow. At midday, during January and February, bald eagles perch all along the river, sometimes on a snagged branch in the middle of its current.

In the morning, I'm outside quickly. R has built a new shed and cut down two or three of the cedars that had died. She's moved the wood-pile. There are several new bird feeders, all carefully placed.

Nuthatch, crow, Canada geese, some sort of sea gull, goldfinch. I take up the habit of noticing again. It's clear and cold and windy, and there are eight eagles soaring and circling. This year they're hanging out in a big, old dead sycamore, its enormous trunk and two main forks weathered white as if lightning struck. By afternoon, there are eighteen. Ten are aloft, circling, first on the other side of the river, then slowly ascending, the circle moving until right above me, sometimes disappearing in the glare, then white flashing. Five others sit in the white tree across the river, and in another tree, one juvenile with two more adults. In late afternoon, they sit on a tree branch snagged in the river, soar over the water at eye level. Every film clip or photograph of bald eagles I see is set in some wild and distant land at high altitude, or in a zoo. Yet here they are with me, along a river just a couple of miles south of a small town in the middle of midwestern farmland.

I had learned to see the birds, but now I wanted to know more. I wanted to understand this place, and its hold on me, more fully—and thereby, as I would later come to see, somehow secure a hold on it.

▲

I walk down the road with Aggie midmorning in January, tired, unsettled. The man who used to live across the road is no longer there. The doghouse and the satellite dish no longer stand guard over the concrete block foundation of the second house on the road. A small shed has been half constructed at the place next door, the one where the fire had been. Nevertheless, I expected to be able to walk the road, to breathe in the solitude, to allow time in the stripped-bare winter to pare away all that had kept me from attending to my soul.

One morning as we approach the spot where the landowner's house sits, set back and raised on a berm, both of his German shepherds are wandering in the road. This is new—I have never seen them off his property unless they're with him. I stop Aggie, we stand staring at each other, and then I turn back. Are we now going to be unable to walk to the head of the road without encountering the only dogs in the area who threaten rather than play? I grit my teeth all day. And the next morning. But we don't encounter them again for weeks.

Several days later, bumping down off the concrete surface of Izaak Walton Road onto the gravel and holes of Camino del Rio late in the afternoon, I smell a wood fire as I see smoke rising from the trees on the left, drifting across the road. The landowner—the man R calls the Termite—has parked his pickup in the road, barely to the side; he's in the woods tending a large pile of burning brush and stumps and whole trunks of trees. The next morning when we walk up the road, the smell lingers in the dried grasses. I can see where tire treads have left the road, where some of the deadfall has begun to be cut up, a woodpile begun. The charred area is a smudge in the snow. Almost every day from then on, I hear or see him and his dogs, sometimes with his son, cutting and clearing and burning. Some mornings the fire is still smoking. One morning the charred spot extends beyond the pile and reaches the road, like a prairie burn. I am never able to discern a pattern to what he has cleared.

This is probably why the German shepherds are now to be seen each morning across the road, wandering out of the brush, venturing farther from the sloping lawn of their house. The land all along the road is his, thick with undergrowth, where there are almost as many fallen trees as standing. Here, two years ago, I had seen dozens of woodpeckers of at least five species. The pile of neatly stacked, evenly sized logs does not grow after that first day. He seems to be cleaning out the underbrush, cleaning up the windfall, but it really never gets any cleaner, and nothing of any usable shape or size is ever cleared out. I cannot figure out what he is up to, but I don't stop to ask. I never meet his eyes, nor receive even a wave in return to my own perfunctory one. Without eye contact, he becomes the Termite to me as well. He is my neighbor, too, of course, but he and his dogs threaten one of the most important ways I have of knowing this place, its dense and layered life. As I walk the road every day, there is now something that sends me back into wariness, alert to threat or intrusion, alert to the boundaries of safety.

Over the weeks and months that winter recedes, I walk the road seeking to let my feet and ears and skin teach me how to see deeper, what to ask, trying to gain for myself a richer understanding of the ecology of this place. Change is inevitable, I know, but it occurs to me that over the time I have been resident on the gravel road at the end of Izaak Walton, in the area I soon learn is variously called the Showers Addition or Picnic Point, all change has been a matter of subtraction and loss.

The marsh, differently

TWO YEARS OF DRY winters have left it empty. Down where the marsh used to be, there are only grasses. We've seen deer in there a couple of times. And the matted-down tunnels in the grass where animals of all sizes have entered off the road. But there has been noticeably less life on Izaak Walton Road. No green herons, no cedar waxwings, far fewer redwing blackbirds, no wood ducks, no barn swallows, no kingfishers, no egrets, no ospreys. No beavers. No surface to ponder or plumb or dive beneath.

Or so I thought.

On Wednesday, it poured. Just poured, on and on. You could hear it on the rooftops of large stores, even inside where canned music was playing and people talking. It pounded layers of caked dust off my car and off all the leaves of shrubs and vines lining the road. It flattened areas of the tallgrass that lay unprotected by any tree branch. It made milky, light-gray puddles in the potholes and in the tire tracks. And it made a stream in the marsh.

It wasn't much of a stream. Tracing the middle, like a seam, a thin line of deeper, greener shoots and stalks, some lined with red, had run back into its depths even when it had appeared to be dry. The morning after the rainstorm, there was visible water, in all about three feet wide.

That morning as I stood and Aggie sniffed at the side of the marsh, there was the distinct and persistent sound of a frog. All spring, there had not been the sound of a frog there at all, and I hadn't actually heard any peepers. A subtle buzzing in the evenings, yes, not quite cicadas, not quite the distinctness of peepers either. But this was definitely a frog, deep and resonant.

The next morning, I almost missed it. Just before the marsh, Aggie started sniffing intently at something in the middle of the road. From a few feet away, I couldn't even tell there was anything there. I quickly checked that it wasn't something she could eat; whatever it was was flattened, so I turned away. But then turned back, because I realized it was dried blood. And then I saw other patches and then a larger one, a flattened, dust-covered, squashed turtle. A small one with a long tail, so it was probably a baby snapper. But a turtle. The color of the dried blood told me that it hadn't been here long, but I also knew because it hadn't been here yesterday morning. It had had no chance here on this road, with the dump trucks going back and forth so frequently; it never would have had time to make it to the other side.

I looked up, wondering how these creatures survive without the marsh, how and where they hunker down. I looked up as two county sheriff's cars, lights flashing, pulled into the head of the road. We stood to the side as they passed, fast and quiet, and went back to looking out into the marsh, my mind split contemplating two questions. One was how the frog and the turtle had lived in the dry marsh, and why only after a rain they had emerged to be seen and heard. The other was about the sheriff's cars and what emergency, crisis, or need had emerged at 6:30 in the morning down Izaak Walton Road.

About the first, I finally came to a hypothesis. It must be that one or more of my assumptions have been wrong. That the marsh had not been dry after all. That deep beneath what I saw, under the grass and shoots, had been water all along. Not water deep enough for a beaver to move around, but enough moisture and mud that frogs and turtles found it possible to live. Yet what would have brought them out, visible and vulnerable to harm, to the forces of the other natures living and working along Izaak Walton Road?

And perhaps they had not been living there at all. Perhaps back beyond the reaches of what I could see, this marsh connected—or lay close by a connection—to the water-filled pits of the quarry. Or to a river inlet. Before the storm, the river level had been dropping steadily, so that a sandbar had appeared on the shore opposite the cabin, on the inside curve of its bend. The river had risen immediately after the storm, pretty full. Wasn't it conceivable that its level affected the moisture in the swamp? Yet the river rose and fell repeatedly over the months, affected more by the decisions on water flow made by the controllers of the dam up at Coralville than by a day's rainfall.

Perhaps the emergency or crisis was only a mistakenly dialed 911, a mistake I myself once made. Perhaps it was someone choking, or a broken-in door. Whatever it was, perhaps it was resolved before the sheriff's cars got there. They were driving back, without lights or passengers, before we were even halfway back down Izaak Walton Road.

I realize I am speculating and imagining, as I have always done, without information and without a clear idea of how to get information. They are neither mysteries nor puzzles, just evidence of the limited ways I have of knowing my world. A reminder of all the things I do not know. And for now, both questions remain, as we step off the pavement onto the gravel, back to the cabin and breakfast.

Accident or refuge

"IT FEELS A LITTLE like the site of some sort of industrial accident," Pam had said when she stopped here on her way across country.

I look up from writing that sentence, glance out one of the large cabin windows. Across the river, two of the bald eagles are large and dark on a bare limb in the canopy of hundreds of trees with their tops snipped off. I breathe in sharply, holding it. I had thought the eagles would be gone by now; last time I lived here, they had left by March. I grab the binoculars, the dog, a hat, gloves, go quietly outside. We walk the dirt road along the river. It is a few degrees above freezing, the snow mush, the road rutted, the sky gray.

I had told Pam about this place—after I lived here the second time, for a full six months—about the birds, the marsh and beaver, the isolation and silence. Pam has encyclopedic knowledge about alternative horticulture, ecological awareness, environmental politics. She is an organic gardener, a worm farmer, a native species enthusiast, a progressive radical peacenik protester grandmother, a good friend with a robust and hearty laugh, a strong sense of justice, and an equal dose of cynicism and optimism in her soul. When I am weighted with despair or paralysis about anything, she is an endless source of cheer and good news; when I am delighted or hopeful about something new, she can be counted on to remind me of some inconvenient fact or perspective I'd been hoping to ignore.

"Like an industrial accident," she said, and I did a double take, wondering how we could be seeing such different things. We had just left the pavement of Izaak Walton Road, were crunching over newly laid gravel on Camino del Rio, passing the silver maple where the barred owls fledged.

In Michigan, I choose the two-lane roads to drive to the city, and when I point to the bronze light of sunset on the mowed fields, Pam talks about how painful it is to see them. It reminds her of the pesticides and herbicides drenching the soil, the grain, and the hands of the farm workers.

I turn to the river and for a few dismal seconds, I realize what it might look like if you hadn't seen it over time, hadn't seen it at dawn or dusk, hadn't stood with the cormorants swooping silently in over you, hadn't stood at midnight in the frigid air in flannel listening to the geese huddled into the river's elbow, or been watched daily by the eagles hanging out on those broken treetops.

Listen to these details again: sand and gravel pits, a field of recycled cars, two concrete plants, a river lined by trees with their tops sheared off. It's not pretty. It has fewer than ten human dwellings on it.

What is going on below the surface of this place? Am I driving the road for the last season before the landowner clear-cuts along both sides? What is it exactly that the sand and gravel company does—does it dig down or will it be expanding, wiping out the other road and its small contingent of houses? What happened to the marsh? What am I looking at when I peer into it—a formerly open waterway now increasingly clogged with invasive and alien vegetation, or a formerly rich wetland being drained by development somewhere else? What is it that brings all the birds here? Why this turn in the river?

And just what does it mean that one man owns the land but individuals own the houses on them? Did I mishear R when she said the lease would eventually revert to the county? What are the legal terms of what is bound to whom?

Is this, as it seemed to me two years ago, a hidden refuge for birds as well as broken spirits, or do I need more of Pam's tutelage to see the poison at its core? Probably neither. I know about the lure of dichotomies and how rarely they hold any truth—probably there is some grain of both, and more, to be found. I read a story in the *New York Times* about what's come back in the Chernobyl region years after the nuclear meltdown. Neglect is a double-edged knife: it allows life to flourish at the same time that it invites or allows transgression, damage. We have not been encouraged to understand these complicated interweavings of systems, how fragile they are in the face of even small interferences.

Pam resumed: "Who was Izaak Walton?" I didn't know.

Later, I went looking. An eighteenth-century British gentleman who wrote a book on fishing. A writer I'd never heard of. Namesake of a conservation organization I knew nothing about. And then I began to realize that there was a lot more that I didn't know about life off Izaak Walton Road, along the dirt and gravel road where the Iowa River bends back upon itself, heading north before it turns south again. Not just the place-names, not just the names and kinds of birds and the wildlife that inhabited the places I didn't see, how it came to be habitat for such a rich range of birds, but also how some of the land came to be quarried and dug up, who tended these places and had owned them, what went on in the transit between dark and dawn, dawn and light, light and dusk.

And so, in the winter and spring of yet another year, with a third opportunity to spend time living in the cabin on the gravel road along the Iowa River, I set out to learn.

Izaak Walton's league

ONCE I STARTED WONDERING about Izaak Walton, I also began
wondering about all sorts of things that I'd been passing every day
along the road. It was well on into spring when I did more than simply
notice the assorted humps in the grass on the Izaak Walton League
lawn. Some resembled animals—a black bear, a turkey—but they were
odd sized and a bit too much like lawn ornaments. Some were just
berms, long, high mounds of earth covered with grass. Far back from
the lawn, where the long drive ended, was a spacious wooden assembly
hall in the shade of a grove of sixty- and eighty-foot oak, sycamore, and
honey locust. I'd never been inside, but I had the feeling I knew what it
was like in there—the smell and the quality of light. In summer heat,
with a keg of beer, the windows unshuttered and doors propped open,
it was probably cool and pleasant, and the floorboards echoed, unless it
was filled with people dancing. I knew it was rented out for weddings,
fund-raisers, family reunions. Nothing fancy at all, just a place to have
a party with enough space there would be no worrying about the noise.
Out front, on that expanse of grass, you'd expect to find a ball field
marked off. The small building is where you'd expect the bases locked
away—a dark-green, windowless wooden cube, electrical wiring and
outside spotlights, a set of steps up to the top, where you'd look for the
scorekeeper. But there were no base paths, and no slats for the score.
Just a barrel for trash and the matted-down grass of tire tracks.

Weeks passed before I walked close enough to inspect this part of
the place and realized it was a practice range for bow shooting. The

bales of hay weren't enough of a clue for me. I had to walk all the way down the drive, back to the hall, then turn around and come back through the grassy field, heading again toward the road. Only then did I walk up to the animal forms, close enough that I could see the pitted sides of each animal. Only from that angle could I see its use: the shooters stood in front of the green cube building and shot toward the road I walked on. The road the school bus came down. The road of the gravel trucks. It left a bad taste in my mouth.

Pam had asked me who Izaak Walton was. I wonder that I had not even wondered. I walk down this road just breathing, just noticing what lives here, what grows here, what has appeared overnight. I wonder if I have blinded myself to most of the human-created elements, but this clearly is not so. I seem simply not to have seen the things I did not want to see—the evidence of destruction, violence, or neglect.

▲

Now when I drive past the Izaak Walton League, the grass is a deep green, and most of the fake animals are gone. The hummocks are still there, also sprouting green. Lately, there have been evenings when a pickup, or several of them, has pulled onto the grass around the green cube. One evening as I was headed out to the Hy-Vee, lights on the two corners of the building were on and the door was open. Later as I drove back down the dark road with the darkened fields on either side, I could see slivers of light coming from gaps around the door, and the shadows of one or two cars. I keep thinking I will stop one day, try to talk to these guys—for all I see are guys—and I wonder how I'll do it and how I'll be received. "Hi. How're you doing? Just wondering what you all do here, what this place is all about."

▲

"We're an environmental organization," says Janet Forbes, the woman I'd been directed to call by the answering machine for the number listed for the Izaak Walton League. I'm hopeful. "We're nonprofit, involved in hunter education, and we work closely with the DNR." At that point in our conversation, she makes a switch I don't notice at first, from first person to third. "They meet the second Tuesday of the month at the building. They do a variety of things—like build wood duck houses, which they give to the public. They make them out of barn board they get. They make about twenty-five a year, usually by the first week in March so people can get them put up in time."

"That large building is the chapter house—the big hall—which they rent out for weddings and such, it's their major source of income. There's the horseshoe pit, for members. But the Ikes usually go out there for the bow and arrow range."

I want to know about the other buildings on the property, all of which I'd seen as I walked around with Aggie in the deserted early mornings.

"The campsites there, well, yeah, they're for the public. Lemme see now, I think it's five dollars a night, and then ten dollars for a weekend. That old cabin is gonna be torn down. It used to be rented out by the year, but it's falling apart. The other house they been using for storage, for the barn board. I don't know, I think it's coming down soon too."

And when I ask about the property, she offers, "Oh well, I'm not sure, it's been there forever. Part of the Wagner Memorial, I heard." Later, I learn that this parcel of land is a gift from yet another old woman. In the Johnson County Recorder's Office, in Transfer Book 219, there is a record of a sale for $1 of a parcel of land on June 4, 1954, from Mayme Wagner, a single woman, to the Wagner Memorial Holding Corporation. She was in Dade City, Florida, when she signed it and it was notarized. It includes this note: "It is understood that all equipment and furnishings in the skating rink and the cottage adjacent thereto shall stay on said premises and become the property of the Wagner Memorial Holding Corp."

▲

I have been asking people if they've heard of Izaak Walton. So far, it's running about fifty-fifty between those who have no recognition of the name, and those who say something like this: "Uh . . . yeah . . . the Izaak Walton League . . . don't they have something to do with the outdoors, like hunting and fishing?" When I follow up with "Yes, but do you know who Izaak Walton was?" almost every person reverts to a blank stare. One says, "Wasn't he British?" And only one person, when I ask, immediately looks at me somewhat taken aback, and says, "Well of course. *The Compleat Angler*. A delightful book. You've read it, of course" (not really a question).

I haven't. Yet. But this man—a professor retired from an English department—assumes it is still standard reading for literature students. I remember that he had once told me of a sad fishing trip with his son. Perhaps he assumes anyone interested in outdoor activities and nature writing, as he knows I am, surely would have read it.

▲

Find a book about fishing and the enjoyment—not the technicalities—of it and you'll almost certainly find a reference to Izaak Walton. *The Compleat Angler* is, apparently, the second most frequently reprinted book in the English language (after the Bible). Ironically, Izaak Walton's book contains, and was informed by, technical information. But it's the people who have come to think of fishing (often with sarcasm and wit) as more than a way to catch dinner, more than a competitive sport, for whom Izaak Walton stands as a kind of father figure. The nature writer Thomas McGuane says that the book "is not about how to fish but about how to *be*." Others talk about fly-fishing as an activity appropriate for musing and meditating. They talk about sitting on the banks of a river with a book in one hand and a rod in the other. It is, to read these fisher folk, a bucolic and pastoral pastime.

All manner of writers, it seems, have weighed in on Izaak over the centuries, with very varied opinions. There's Washington Irving:

For my part, I was always a bungler at all kinds of sport that required either patience or adroitness, and had not angled for above half an hour before I had completely "satisfied the sentiment," and convinced myself of the truth of Izaak Walton's opinion, that angling is something like poetry—a man must be born to it. I hooked myself instead of the fish; tangled my line in every tree; lost my bait; broke my rod; until I gave up the attempt in despair, and passed the day under the trees, reading old Izaak; satisfied that it was his fascinating vein of honest simplicity and rural feeling that had bewitched me, and not the passion for angling.

There is, on the other hand, Lord Byron, who was no fan of fishing. He called Walton a "sentimental savage" who should have the tables turned on him:

Whatever Izaak Walton sings or says;
The quaint, old, cruel coxcomb, in his gullet
Should have a hook, and a small trout to pull it.

The book, he says, teaches "the art of angling [as] the cruelest, the coldest, and the stupidest of all pretend sports."

▲

Some of the same large differences of opinion and taste regarding the type of outdoors enthusiasts that now park their pickups on the newly mowed grass of the Johnson County chapter of the Izaak Walton League property apparently attached themselves to the book Izaak Walton wrote. What Byron said may also be said, in less lyrical language, about hunters, be they bowhunters, shotgun hunters, trappers, or high-powered rifle hunters on the savannas of eastern Africa. The same kind of imagination that Byron put to verse, wishing the deed done unto the doer, still finds its way today into environmental and activist tracts and websites and public forums. I have probably indulged in it myself. The same irony embodied by Izaak Walton's book and its reception over the centuries is evident today, even in as simple an exchange as mine with Janet Forbes. Those who kill or harvest creatures from the wild are very often the ones who do the work to tend the environment, the wild places. Ducks Unlimited, Whitetails Unlimited, Pheasants Forever, the Izaak Walton League, the Michigan United Conservation Clubs—the list is long. And they write about it too.

Wildlife biologists and researchers have taught me to understand that any environmental policy—any public policy regarding natural resources—must take into account the needs, desires, and uses of multiple stakeholders. Some of us, in other words, use wild places to contemplate, observe, walk through, and learn; some of us use them to contemplate, observe, walk through, learn, and harvest, honing skills that, among other things, become building blocks for foundational values later in life, to judge from the way so many writers recount their early experiences in the wild.

▲

During the weeks that I was reading Izaak Walton's book, alongside all the writers who have had something to say about his book, there was a decided increase in the activity on the property of the Johnson County chapter of the Izaak Walton League. Nearly every evening, there were pickups parked outside the clubhouse and guys milling about, each with an elbow bent. Sometimes there was a fire in a pit, and sometimes a light would be shining from inside.

In the mornings, I would walk by, craning my neck. Sometimes, if the night had been mild, the sun strong enough, the grass not too wet, and if there were no remaining pickups or tents, I walked across the well-mowed grassy lawn to get a closer look. The horseshoe pits had been tended. Long-handled barbecue implements lay across the top of the long, closed-top cooker. One morning, I found long metal arrows sticking into several badly deformed target animals. I pulled one out, examined the barbs, put it back in, and turned the image over in my head all the way back to the cabin.

Another morning, the door to the clubhouse stood wide open. Not a single truck or car to be seen, no tent, and as far as I could tell, no one sleeping on any of the lawn chairs hanging around in various unusable positions. I couldn't resist a peek inside.

Aggie sniffed and prodded around the cooker while I stood on the doorstep. It really was a clubhouse, the kind you might imagine that boys grown up might make for themselves. There was a bag of potatoes, a microwave, potholders, wire cutters, and a lot of other junk on the counters and walls. It wasn't so much dirty as it was a mess. What drew my attention was a bulletin board just inside the door. I never did step foot over the threshold—I want to be clear that I did not physically intrude—but my eyes kept being drawn to the photographs stapled to the board. Twice, as I turned to go, leaving my dew-wet shoe print on the doorsill, I turned back to examine them more closely. The face of a young girl, wide open in joy holding a small fish, kept hold of me. The rest were almost entirely of men holding carcasses— multiple turkeys, multiple white-tailed deer, many with their black eyes open as if staring at the camera. Almost all the photographs were slightly discolored, as if years had passed or the film had been old, and a lot of them were blurry. In one, a man holds his arms wide, grasping the ends of the wings of what is obviously a large bird, but try as I might—and I don't know why I kept trying—I couldn't tell what the bird was, because where the head should have been was a white blur. My mind of course was running on overdrive, and my heart hurt. Why would someone keep the evidence of having done this? Was it perhaps no endangered or protected bird but some nuisance, something common? How would I know? Who could tell? By evening when I drove past again, the door was once more shut and locked, a new black-and-neon-orange sign blazing "Whitetails Unlimited" out across the field to the road.

Rescue

PERHAPS, I TELL MYSELF each morning as I walk, it would be useful to say it out loud, simply and directly, and then try to explain.

I am a rescuer.

I drive interstate thruways and residential curves alert, tense, looking for what might run into the road. From a quarter mile away, I can spot what I know will be a cat sitting in the tallgrass of a highway divide, streams of death on either side. I brake for squirrels on country roads and city streets, and according to friends who have been along with me, I talk to them as well, then honk and wait. Get out of the road! Don't you know this is not safe? I have stopped for countless animals that have been hit and injured. The staff at the veterinary school's wild animal clinic know me well; I have brought in sparrow nestlings with eyes not yet open, baby rabbits barely breathing. While friends held their dogs at bay, I once ran circles around an abandoned baseball field, peeling off my outer shirt in order to catch a limping squirrel. I carried it a dozen blocks to my car, then drove to the clinic. I have taken stray dogs to the shelter. I have taken stray dogs into my garage until I could find their homes, or any home, enduring sleepless nights as they shredded and chewed everything in the garage. I took home a cat from under the deck of a downtown restaurant, where she had been dumped, pregnant.

I am a rescuer. I often enough find myself trying to rescue humans too, despite the warnings in books on codependency and addiction recovery. In those books, the label is not very flattering, not intended as a positive personality trait. Their descriptions probably apply to my regrettable habit of freely and quickly offering advice to my sisters, to friends, to total strangers. I try to help. As a therapist once explained to me, and as I myself promptly explain to anyone else possessed of the same habit, it does not work. It is not very respectful of the other person. It assumes that they cannot fend for themselves. It is condescending and presumptuous. I recognize this and I am trying to change.

But not with animals. In human relationships, the situations into which rescuers swoop, wanting to fix, are less often dangerous than troublesome—knotty relationships and unproductive behaviors. When it comes to animals, however, I am in the grip of a deep and urgent need, a compulsion. It is, I believe, about life and death. We are responsible, I will tell you in order to convert you to the same urgency and action. We must protect, I will insist, domesticated as well as wild animals, which cannot survive in human-altered environments without human care.

I am a rescuer, and apparently have always been one.

It's a complicated weaving of forces that compels me. I try to unravel some of them. During my elementary school summers, my brother and sister and I had the habit of leaving the house while my parents still slept, sometimes before sunrise, sometimes in warm gray mist, to ride our bikes up and down the streets of our neighborhood, venturing far because there was no traffic, no one to warn us otherwise. We rode and shushed each other, giggling, swerving, daring one another. On a side street one day, we came upon four newborn kittens in the gutter. No mother, no owner, no adult to ask. I'm pretty sure I wouldn't have listened anyway; I did not trust adults to have reliable answers or plans for taking care of small, vulnerable beings. Within minutes, they were snuggled in the basket of my bike, then home in our backyard tucked into a doll carriage. By the evening of that same day, the sun still strong, I was sitting on the sofa in our living room, sobbing as my mother and a neighbor tried to explain that taking them to "the pound" had been the best and only thing to do, that we couldn't keep them, couldn't raise them. I was inconsolable because they had already taken them, without telling me. I knew that my father hated cats, and I knew that "the pound" was where they killed animals. My adult compulsion may be an attempt, over and over, to rewrite that story, to undo that earlier loss, to counter what I took to be the failure of the adults around me to protect what was young and vulnerable. More likely, it was my attempt to rewrite the story of my very own young self that needed rescuing and protecting from several secret violations as well as a variety of very public and visible ones.

I return to the question raised for me by Pam's comment: Is this a place of neglect or refuge? I walk the road aware of the complicated interweavings of ecosystems, and of individuals, how fragile they are. My impulse to rescue is an old psychodrama. I despair and rage in the face of systemic injustices of sexism, racism, economic oppression, homophobia, environmental destruction. The ecosystem may survive, species may flourish or move elsewhere. But individuals are sacrificed in the meantime.

This morning I rescued three snails and one frog on the road. I rescued them from certain death by truck tire. I know this because there was one frog and one turtle for whom I was too late. I'd been walking toward the head of the road, the sun at my back warming me enough that I took off my shirt, tying the arms around my waist. A white pickup turned and came down the road. I expected it to be the one I usually meet in the mornings—with double tires in the back, its rear wheel wells bulging, overdosed on steroids. The driver, unlike all the other drivers that I pass on this road, raises his fingers in the Iowa country two-finger wave when we pass. That he acknowledges me at all is one of the two things that make him different; the other is that he keeps to a slow speed, much slower than others.

I'm not sure it would have made a difference if it had been that white pickup that came past me this morning. After Aggie and I had reached the head of the road and turned back, walking toward the sun glaring off the pavement still wet from the predawn rain, I came upon the frog and bent to look more closely. Its belly was still covered with the lizard-like skin that let me know it had indeed been a frog. But its splayed legs had no skin, just exposed leg muscles attached to tendon and bone, glistening in the sun, still pink and perfect, as if I were standing over a dissecting table.

Although it had been raining for the past several nights, there wasn't any more water visible in the marsh than there had been all spring. As I walked on, I saw the flattened turtle. It wasn't the one I'd seen the other day after the big storm—whatever bits of it were left after a couple days of being pounded by the truck tires would surely have been washed off the road already. This turtle had probably been killed yesterday—another small snapper, I think, but I cannot be certain because its head and front legs were gone; its tail was there, as long as its shell, which was all of about five inches.

A little farther on was another belly-up frog, this one larger and whole. I saw movement on the delicate yellow of its throat. Light flickering through the willow branches? I bent closer. No—it was alive. I turned it over. The eyes were open wide, the spots on its back were shiny, no marks or tears that I could see. It sat. In the road. I poked its butt. "Get out of the road," I said. It hopped once, falling over on its shoulder. A broken leg? Then why was it lying belly up? I prodded again. It hopped and fell over onto its back again, lying there. I picked it up and righted it. It sat. It hopped. It was headed for the road again. I picked it up again and set it in the grass and started to walk on. I went back and put it deeper into the grasses at the side of the road in the dew-covered shade, headed for the ditch, then walked away.

There's only so much you can do to help a creature in distress, even if you are a rescuer. Perhaps it was ready to die, I thought as I headed back down the road, eyes scanning the ground ahead of me. Perhaps that's what they do when they're old and dying. What else could it be? Perhaps I wasn't really helping at all. Perhaps it was something frogs do, like possums who play dead, exposing themselves to further danger as they lie in the road. How do you know if you are helping or not in these chance encounters of a life? I could be an unwitting pawn. I imagined the voice-over in a cartoon: "Oh no, oh no, here she comes again, run!" Or on my better days, "Hey, here she comes—quick, go play dead in the road!"

We drifted to the left side of the road as another pickup passed us headed for the gravel pit gate. Ahead of me, I saw a snail. I bent and picked it up with two fingers, tossing it lightly into the ditch. Fifty yards farther on, another one. Each was about the size of my fingernail. How many others had I missed? Hard to say. How many had already been crushed? What is the place of snails in the ecology of the marsh and fields and woods along this road, and between this road and the river? There must be thousands of them. Behind the Los Angeles apartment house I lived in years ago, there was a narrow wooded path where I had walked my dog. There were days when the snails were so thick along the path beneath the tall, papery eucalyptus trees that you couldn't step without crushing several at a time. Clearly, they were a problem. I made jokes about French cuisine. But these here along this road in Iowa surely can't be considered a pest, I thought, they must be some other creature's dinner.

My own ignorance distresses me. I'm sure there are people I can consult who would tell me about the way they study an ecological space such as this, taking samples from one cubic meter every so often, then extrapolating. I'm sure by these methods they would be able to tell me how dense is the population of snails, what their place is in the food chain, how turtles live and where, how frogs live with the fluctuations of water levels, what's affecting the level of the marsh this year, how that changes the number of herons, who no doubt feed on the snails and the frogs.

But I've also heard biologists or conservation officers speak often enough about things like overbreeding as an adaptation to counteract predation. Abundance means there's plenty to spare, enough to write off to truck tires and suburban sprawl. Once, after speeding past a Canada goose and her brood of goslings standing ready to cross several lanes of interstate, I phoned the DNR to give their location and ask them to intervene. How hard is it to stop the traffic for a few minutes? "We aren't going to do anything about that, ma'am," answered the officer on duty. "They're urban dwellers and a certain number of them are going to succumb to urban risks." This willingness to write off individuals is enough to send me out walking roads and driving highways looking for strays and accidents about to happen.

Why bother? I imagine the guy in the next pickup asking.

One answer is this: I do it because the small things of life are so often defenseless against the violence and brutish ignorance of the world. Because I will not be the person who walks by and refuses to see cruelty or injustice, refuses to speak or take action. While contemplation of how those forces play out on historical and global stages is enough to keep me paralyzed with the bedcovers over my head, here is a way and a place, in this small corner of the world, where I can act. They are admittedly small gestures, possibly ineffectual and mock-heroic, poor substitutes for countering war and bigotry. And yet, my small voice cries "no!" when I am faced with what appears to me to be imminent death or maiming.

I also do it because although I know what happens on the roadbed when a multi-ton truck meets soft flesh, I do not know what goes on out there in the marsh. The roadbed is merely the exposed part of the life along this stretch of land and riverside. I toss those snails, lightly, into the ditch, also as an offering, as repentance for my ignorance.

I wonder about these things, but I don't pursue answers. Because I also have a complicated relationship to knowledge and knowing. The many field guides to birds and wild flowers on my shelves testify to that. I know, too, that factual information can, at times, interfere with what I know in my bones, in my breathing, in the internal rhythms by which I know when the sun will break the horizon. In my ability to know there's something in the branches, in the thicket, before I know I've seen it. Facts and statistics will not help me know the life of this marsh or this riverbank or this ditch or this stand of willow. What I want is to be able to see them—moving, interacting, feeding. I want to know the life cycle of that particular frog. I want to know exactly where the herons roost. I want to know where the turtles came from—the exact place—and how this one climbed out onto the road. I want to see what is happening at night, where the barred owl flies over and in which tree it waits. I want to know where the water is in that marsh, how deep it is there in the middle where the pencil line of dark green runs down its spine. I want to know what else is living in there that I have never seen. I want to be a part of this ecology, a part that knows its place and role. Facts and statistics will not give me what I really want.

I am caught, stuck in an untenable position, in a contradiction I have repeatedly turned away from examining too closely. I want to know this place without interfering, without marking it or taking from it. At the same time, I cannot bear standing by and not involving myself. When I tell myself I am interfering for the good, I also hear a voice that asks, Whose good? Can we ever know fully what impact our footprint makes? After the Exxon Valdez spill, and then the Deepwater Horizon spill, a wildlife biologist friend complained to me what a waste it was to spend so much time and money cleaning each sea otter and gull, time and money that could have been so much better spent managing ecosystems for long-term survival of the species. But people, he said, feel better caring for individuals.

I want to believe my presence is benign and that my actions are taken to preserve this place to which I am so deeply connected, a place on which I know I have no hold, no claims, neither property owner nor voting resident. A nagging fear persists nevertheless that by rescuing, I am interfering. Perhaps in returning the frog to the underbrush, I had interrupted a predator now waiting and watching from the wings, somewhere out of my sight—or, more likely, clearly within my sight, were I knowledgeable enough to see it. Perhaps, as with people, rescuing is in fact an act of disrespect, a lack of faith that the ecosystem is healthy enough to sustain itself. I can comfort myself with this truth for a time, and then what comes back to me is a single cry, a single pair of eyes, the single one here and now in front of my feet, this one's fear, this danger and this need. Perhaps, then, my actions are less about preserving the road and marsh and river and—once again— much more about working free of my own past.

I tossed the snails lightly back into the ditch, turned the frog over and headed it toward the marsh, sending them back into the under-belly of life in this place, back to a life and a fate out of my own sight line. I did it because in helping life off Izaak Walton Road to continue to flourish, in its way, off the roadbed, keeping out of sight, I am caring for the small, the vulnerable, the wounded part of myself.

Roadkill

THIS TIME WHEN I live in the cabin off Izaak Walton, I walk the road wanting to see and understand the complex relationships among things. But the full picture, once I start prying and pushing deeper, is not pretty. It now does appear at times to be a place of neglect, the waste pile or armpit the city doesn't expect anyone to care about. Or is it a refuge because it is neglected? Riparian zones are understood as rich ecological niches. Any place along a river, anywhere, is likely to be coveted territory. The ecology of this riparian zone along this river does not include much human activity—not compared to the way riverfront property is developed so rapaciously in most places. It does include, nevertheless, an artery of death.

After a rain in early spring, we go out and on up the road. My rubber soles stumble on the rocks and gravel more easily than my heavy-soled boots of winter. Sticks in the road, I am thinking as I pick my way around them—stuff knocked off the trees by the storm's wind—and at the same time, I am wondering. Even where there are no trees lining the road? And all the same size? Like the three- or four-inch catkins from a walnut or white oak, littering the ground.

But they're not. They're worms. Hundreds, no, thousands of them, stretched out, some leaving tunneled trails in the dirt marking their paths across the road. Most are dead, squashed. Some still wriggle and progress. My feet come down next and next and next and I try not to do more damage. But it is 6:30 a.m.—by 7:00, at least two cars will have bumped over all this on their way to work, and there's no way those tires will be careful.

By the next morning, there's no sign of any of them. None. How is that possible, even if robins and starlings and jays had feasted nonstop for a day and night?

▲

A massacre of frogs. Most of them not squashed. Some whole and undamaged. All turned belly up, stiff legged, extended. A hot, steamy morning already at 6:00 a.m. These days I start out with T-shirt and an overlarge, long-sleeved oxford shirt, until the sun comes up, until we're to the head of Camino del Rio, onto the more exposed stretch of Izaak Walton Road. No shade, the sun fully up by then.

One morning we come upon at least six frogs, each about three inches long, together in one spot on the road. Medium sized. Not the thumbnail ones I see usually at the last minute, then cup in my hand, and move off into the roadside brush; not the ones that must be huge, belching through the beaver marsh. Extended, these are just the size of my middle finger. All of them. What has done this? I haven't a clue.

A few days later, dozens of them, all over the road.

▲

A day late in June, past the solstice. When I drive down Izaak Walton Road at dinnertime, I pass a large mess in the middle of the concrete—a turtle, I figure as I aim tires to straddle it. A snapper probably, given the long, pointed tail that I imagine I see amid the bloody mess. In the morning, Aggie and I walk toward the beaver marsh; I want to take a closer look. But I can tell from far off that it isn't there anymore. And I start thinking about the massacres of frogs. And the bit of squashed something I'd passed over another evening a few weeks ago, and how I'd intended to take a closer look, too, the next morning. And how nothing was there.

But what did they do with the shell, Aggie? I ask out loud. I find bits of bone, one small clean, milky, round bit of cartilage, like a knee, something squashed that could have been a few toes. Some slivers of something. And like the crime scene investigators on television last night, I'm wanting tweezers to pick it up, a specimen bag to preserve it, a microscope and expert to identify it. As in so many other things on Izaak Walton Road, I have to make do with speculating.

I think it's bits of shell. So some tire went over it, which isn't surprising, since the dark-green pickup driven by the wizened bean pole of a guy arriving every morning around six to open the gravel pit gate had to have passed over it. I'm guessing a raccoon made a good dinner out of it. Why do I say "a" raccoon? I know they travel so often in groups—it had to have been a bunch of them out here in the road, in the dark, making off with dinner. Still, what did they do with the shell?

▲

In the middle of the road, at the joining of the fork tines of Camino del Rio and the road with no name, on the pavement of Izaak Walton, a lone, dead cardinal. It appears midday. Not squashed, but dusty, battered. By morning, it, too, is gone.

▲

Yet another gray dawn, already heavy. Just past the mailboxes, on the curve, large drops of blood. Still red, soaked into the steel-gray dust. They are evenly spaced and lead from the inside edge of the curve, across the road to its outside edge. Eventually, they shrink in size a bit, but still red, still clearly, identifiably fresh. I am alarmed. I search the brush they lead to—it's high roadside grasses, vines, and shrubs and a few large trees, the uncleared land between Camino del Rio and the few dwellings on the other tine of the fork. In winter, I can see lights through the trees. One year, two dogs lived there and every morning came barking through the brush and torn wire fencing to greet us. Nothing to be learned now without venturing into that thicket, so I go back to the evidence. Large plops of life. Because they are evenly spaced, I deduce it must come from something walking, not dropping from the sky. They begin at one spot in the road—nothing leads to them, only away, into the brush. Injury leads to cover, a hiding place, not into the open. There's nothing more I can figure to do but look around. There's only so far I want to follow where my imagination is heading. It frightens and saddens me.

▲

By the time I'm headed back down the road, toward the cabin, the sun is high enough to cause squinting. From the head of the road, down into the cool tunnel of trees, I'm headed straight into it. It pours and diffuses pale yellow down the chute. This morning, my eyes catch squidges of shimmer, as if a child had decorated the road with a sparkle pen. I know that sign. I bend to find, blended into the yellow-gray roadbed, a perfectly spiraled shell and inhabitant, its brown antennae reaching ahead. Four of them, no more than that, like points on an Etch A Sketch, like frilleries of glitter. I pick up each, no bigger than my thumbnail, and place it on something green, the leaves of a plantain or anemone, out of the road, though not necessarily, I know, out of harm.

Two days later, I'm sitting at the yellow table and I hear a large, slow motor coming down the road. There are only two houses past this one and I know their cars. This isn't one of them. Sounds like slow-moving heavy equipment. Finally, a large yellow tractor-type contraption appears through the trees, its blade down. For some reason I cannot fathom, it is scraping the road, pulling up the larger rocks that had been pressed down into the gravel bed, unsettling the packed dirt so that now it is loose and fine. The next morning, all the roadside weeds and saplings and trees and shrubs are covered with gray powder, shaded in unison. If there are any snails in the road, they are now well buried, well camouflaged, thoroughly crushed.

Garbage

ONE MORNING, I TAKE a small plastic garbage bag with me as I leave the house. Down on Izaak Walton Road, on the hard-top, where at 6:30 the dump trucks start lumbering and rumbling back and forth, often in twos and threes, I have been noticing intrusions of color, flashes of silver along the perimeters and in the ditches. This morning, I head down the road intending to pick up the trash and recycle the pop cans. It's a small thing I can do. I can't retrieve the rusted skeleton of a washing machine that's been in the ditch for at least two or three years, near where the beaver dam used to be. And I'm not going down into those ditches to pull out the trash that has wound its way deep in there, most of it unidentifiable and already disintegrating, some already in twisty-tied bags that sprouted over the winter. I'm sticking to the stuff on the side of the road, nesting among the bindweed, the plantain, the nettles and nut grass.

We are out, Aggie and I, by 5:45, long before anyone's leaving for work or heading out to catch the school bus. We walk up to the head of the road, where Izaak Walton meets old 218. Sun is just reaching the treetops behind us when we turn back and I start bending to retrieve. Heavy with the same dew that feeds the purslane and pokeweed rooted in the roadside gravel, the objects I place in the bag speak a pattern. Cans and plastic bottles of pop. Balls of crushed aluminum fast-food wrappers. Foam cups, clear plastic cups, deep-red plastic cups from Casey's, a fitted lid, and a straw stuck out the top. Rim-cracked fitted lids with no cup in sight. Small foam plates. Candy wrappers, empty bags of cupcakes, chips, cheese puffs.

All these I imagine blown out a window, dropped casually, falling from precarious and neglected perches. I want to believe in the accidentalness of it all, as random as the vegetation sprouting from seeds dropped by overflying birds. Yet I cannot see the empty cigarette packs, fisted and small, as anything but thrown, a conscious gesture, deliberate, dirty, angry. And then I have to face it. I have to listen to what observation is telling me, in the same way that I move back and forth between field guide and roadside grasses or wild flowers, sifting through identifying features, looking for the pattern and the key. This detritus of lunch and midmorning breaks that's too quickly filling and bulging this bright-yellow bag I carry reveals not accident, not the forgetfulness of celebration nor the carelessness of youthful ardor, but a deliberate, patterned mindlessness about this bit of road.

I look around and try to see with other eyes. I follow the trucks from some construction site on the other edge of town, pulling out onto the four-lane highway, through the stoplight traffic in town, turning onto an empty two-lane road, turning then onto this dead-end nothing of a concrete wasteland to the white gate, to the weigh pad, to the yellow fill chute, then lumbering back out to the head of the road, back to the site, back and forth all day.

This third of a mile stretch of road that I know in its small, quiet daily changes, its predawn secrets, its inhabitants hidden by midmorning, shows nothing of itself to the men who ride high above it in dusty cabs. By the time I reach the Izaak Walton League's mailbox, the story of Izaak Walton Road that has been growing for me week by week, through seasons' passing and daily sightings, has changed. I had assumed most of the trash would be from people who rent the League for weekend graduation and wedding parties, and from teenage couples in low-slung cars or rusting pickups who figure they've discovered a dark, deserted road. I had figured that most of what I'd pick up would tell that story. That it would be like the last thing I find that morning, in front of the Izaak Walton bow practice range: a bright-red stretch tube top, too clean, too new, etched with a single tire tread, in sand. The sand that collects on the side there, near where the full dump trucks, turning left too fast, spill their tops. Even folded over and flattened on the roadbed, its small circumference is suggestive, of innocence, of flowering, of the risks of heading down a dark gravel road, of the danger of ending up in a ditch. One morning in late winter, before the snack trash began to appear, I saw a single white condom on this side of the road, folded over in just the same way as this bit of clothing. As I move on, toward what now feels like the relative safety of the gravel road where no trucks or strangers venture, what I leave lying by the side of the road is like a flag, that bit of red fabric tied to the end of cargo sticking out the back of a truck, a warning of the danger you might not perceive until it's too late.

Target

EARLY MAY, 6:20 A.M. It's a warm Saturday morning. Last evening when I drove in, there were several pickups around the clubhouse building at the Izaak Walton League. The light was on, men were standing around, but there were also a couple of tents set up off to the side. That's the first time this season. I wonder if the campers are the Ikes, and if not, what the campers think of the fact that what had seemed a quiet, secluded site when they set up had become a beer-drinking, horseshoe-clanging gathering spot.

Aggie and I get to the head of the road, move out onto the paved Izaak Walton Road, pass the line of trees. In front of a third tent, there's a fire still going. Smoke and a few flames. Lingering from last night or newly started by an early riser? I see no one moving. But there's a deer standing near the horseshoe pit—a target, I now know, carved from foam and painted in muted shades. A couple of other foam targets have appeared in the past few days, and there are signs that someone has been cleaning up the remains of the old turkey and raccoon. The deer is set by the fire and the tents, facing them, not out in front of the clubhouse or by the berms where the targets had previously been set. It's a reminder to me that danger lurks, though not this early. I want to send it away.

The rising sun heats up my back as I continue on. I turn my head, look to the other side of the road, and there at the back of the field of corn stubble, near a swath of lime-green saplings that look like aspen, two deer. Real deer, grazing the stubble. I stop, turning my head from one side of the road to the other. The real thing, early risers; the target, the stand-in, hovering over the sleeping men. You craft the one in order to practice for the other. You sleep while the real quarry tiptoes around you.

I'm the one, however, that the deer are worried about. I'm the one moving, and so is Aggie. I walk slowly, holding irony in either hand, in both hands. These deer are safe.

Two or three mornings later, out on Riverside Drive, a dead deer—not arrow hit but road killed—by the side of the road.

Johnson County Quarry

HERE'S ANOTHER PIECE OF information that started to change the story about Izaak Walton Road for me.

Next to the long drive that leads back to the Izaak Walton League's buildings, there's another long drive running parallel. Two signs hang together at the entrance: Johnson County Auto Recycling and Johnson County Quarry.

Maybe it's the fact that a hundred feet or so down the road, there's a sign that says "City of Iowa City," marking what must be a city boundary. Maybe because the "pond" that's next to the long drive looks like the "sump" of my childhood—a dangerous place at the end of a neighborhood's streets and next to the schoolyard, fenced off and forbidden, dug deep and not pretty at all. Maybe it was an unconscious contrast I drew because everything on the other side of Izaak Walton Road is privately owned. Whatever the reason, I had assumed that Johnson County Quarry was owned by the county.

A tight voice, slightly gravelly, not very deep, answers the phone. I figure my call will be harmless and quick. "I'm curious," I say, "because I walk down that road, can you tell me when the quarry first came into being?"

"Who are you?" Wary. Pointed. "You rent from Southwick? Or are you on the other side there?" OK, so he knows not just Izaak Walton Road but the private property and roads beyond. I tell him I'm renting a place down the road, that I walk every day and I'm just curious.

It turns out that Johnson County Quarry is a private business, owned "by an individual—I can't say a name," he says. "There was a different entrance long ago, but we have more sand and dirt than S&G over there. They're gonna run out and we're not."

I'm struggling to figure out how to navigate this conversation. I'm not even sure what I want to know. Almost all the other conversations I've had with people about this area and its history have blossomed from my first few simple questions into long exchanges, generously shared by people who seem pleased to tell the stories they know. I'm also curious now, wondering about these two companies in the same business right across the road from each other.

"Well, I'm just curious," I repeat. "I've passed by the sign and the pit, but I've never gone down that road there, so I didn't know."

"And you can't go down there. It's illegal."

I start to explain again, but I'm interrupted. "I gotta go now. You don't have to worry no more," the voice says, and hangs up.

I wasn't worried, I want to say to the dead receiver, assuming he'd misunderstood. And then I am. But I'm not sure of what. The next morning, I sling my leg over the gate and walk down the long road. It borders the pond—a pit, really—in which mallards and Canada geese land in winter. Five or six different kinds of wild grasses line the wire fence between this drive and the one to the Izaak Walton League. On this side, at the end, a cattle grate keeps Aggie from coming farther with me, and beyond it sits a very dilapidated trailer with a big sign on the door: No Trespassing. An old brown Volvo butts up against it. The drive curves around and heads straight for what looks like a good while before it snakes again out of my sight. I consider going down it to explore further, but I decide what I'd learn isn't worth the anxiety I am now feeling about this stretch off Izaak Walton Road.

Izaak and I, fishing

"SO, HOW'D YOU DO? Did we hook you?"

It is a cloud-free, seventy-degree Saturday afternoon at F. W. Kent State Park. I have come to the DNR's annual free fishing clinic. Brad takes the fiberglass rod and reel that I hand over, secures the hook on the reel, wipes the rod, and stows it in an aluminum frame triple-decker pole holder. I appear to be the last to return my gear. All the rest—a large gaggle of eight- and ten-year-old boys—have already tossed theirs in the vicinity of the card table and scrambled over to peek into the tanks jammed and piled into the back of the pickup where another DNR guy is preparing to give a little talk about the fish in Iowa's rivers and lakes. The plastic tanks are small and the fish, some of them, are huge.

▲

The first and only time I ever tried to catch a fish was some fifty-five years ago, in a pond in New York City's Central Park, where my grandmother had taken me and my older cousin, Eddie. I can't have been any older than five at the time. We sat on rocks and bare dirt and were pretty much alone. My memory is a snapshot, a moment stilled in time and brevity, neither particularly pleasant, other than in its absence of trauma, nor particularly unpleasant, although I remember something about putting a worm on a hook. Was I worried about killing the worm? Did I catch anything? Was I pleased at being able to perform a task competently? Nothing other than the fact of being there stays with me. Central Park is in the middle of one of the busiest, most densely populated and constructed environments on the planet, and yet I knew it then to be a place of calm.

It's not as if I didn't have opportunities, growing up near water, on an island, close to the shore. Although it's primarily thought of as the suburbs of the greater New York metropolitan area, it is still an island, no spot more than thirty minutes from a shore. My father and his father regularly fished with men from their lodge. All the fishing they did was in ocean and bay waters. We ate fish almost every Friday. There are several photographs of my brother at age six or seven, having returned from a fishing trip with our father, standing in the driveway in plaid flannel shirt and rolled up jeans. He has a fishing pole in one hand, upright like a spear, a fish in the other, a grin on his face, and anywhere from five to ten fish lined up on the asphalt at his feet.

Now my brother, the father of two young boys, lives in Los Angeles and takes his sons fishing. My nephews seem to have a gift for it. From a very young age, whenever Kyle would stick a pole in the water, he'd catch something. Nick's passion is frogs more than fish. Put those boys near water and they become like little men—quiet, contemplative, bent to the task of catching. At holidays and birthdays, the gifts they ask for and receive sound the same note: fishing licenses, fishing poles, lures, reels, bait; things with fish on them, fish books fish hats fish shirts fish ornaments and plaques and photographs.

"Can you believe this is a job?" bursts out Brad, the one with the curly, sandy hair, when I thank him for running the clinic. "I could do this all day, every day."

When I ask about the assorted gear, Brad is the one who steps to the pickup and whips a canvas tarp off four layers of compartmented boxes filled with multicolored small stuff—lures and bobbins and hooks and plastic worms and spinners, and other things with names

I've forgotten. Painted and signed plastic fake fish with three and four hooks embedded in them. One box for fishing the Mississippi. One for muddy, slow-moving streams. Some for when he goes up to the Boundary Waters. One with a hook smaller than the nail on my pinkie finger. Several each for catfish, trout, bass. He goes on but my mind is turning over. I will never, I know, use this much equipment for this many kinds of fish or this variety of conditions. But he's right—there's something seductive about all those colors and names and shapes, organized, categorized, like a buffet, like a vending machine or a candy counter behind glass. I could find myself fishing just for the pleasure of scanning and fingering the choices, reciting their names, trying them out.

It's true, I'm circling with interest, nibbling at the prospect, but not quite hooked, not the way these guys are, and not the way those young boys are, yelping at each catch, running with it or after it. The enterprise still both attracts and repels me. I abhor the pursuit and catching and killing of a life, an act of conquest, for the sport of it. Yet like Washington Irving and probably a host of other people over the years, I'm drawn to the idea of fishing, the leisure, the quiet, the connection through a string and pole between me and something barely seen, below the surface.

I had been reading *The Compleat Angler*. I had been trying to understand the fishers and hunters of the Izaak Walton League better. I had been working to learn more about all that I observed and heard and knew about life on the Iowa River as it bends twice near Izaak Walton Road, bends twice like the shape of the mark that editors use to mean switch two things into each other's place. After listening to what I'd been learning about Izaak Walton, Pam had said to me, "If you want to learn more about living on this river, you have to go fishing on it, you know." And even as I shot back, "Oh, give me a break, will you?" I knew that her needling would stick with me. I could read all I wanted, but Pam knew and I knew the limitations of that kind of knowledge. I had to have at least some small bit of knowing lodged in my limbs and senses. The problem was I did not have any equipment, knew no one in Iowa who fished, and did not have a way to get onto the river. Then I read about the fishing clinic, held every year the first weekend in June. Even though it would be on a lake, not the river, at least I'd get a chance to fish, and perhaps get to listen to some people who fish. But in my blithe willingness to substitute a lake for the river, you will already have noticed the extent of my ignorance in the matter.

Had I been required to read *The Compleat Angler* for a literature class at any point in my college or postgraduate studies, likely as part of a survey of seventeenth-century British literature, I would not, in fact, have finished it. I'd have tried, I'd have begun, and then I am pretty sure that I'd have fallen asleep. Izaak Walton was not considered important enough, by literary scholars, except as he provided some color, a minor figure, a curiosity.

I'd have had no way of conjuring a mental picture, nor a sense of its cultural context, nor, it turns out, any notion of the true legacy of Izaak Walton. And so I read him at this time needing to know about fishing and not to achieve mastery of literary history. I learned, for one thing, that his influence has been wide and persistent. I also learned, from his enthusiastic and gentle extolling of the virtues of "angling," that the difference between fly-fishing and fishing with a reel is among the things that people who love fishing pay attention to and argue about.

It was Izaak Walton who led me to begin to see fishing as more than a metaphor, more than a theme for gift giving, more than a guy thing. It was Izaak Walton who had led me to this point, ready to pick up pole and worm on the edge of water.

▲

"I know nothing about this," I say to the two guys from the DNR sitting at the table, and hold out my empty hands.

"Clay'll fix you right up, then," says Brad, rounded at the belly with twinkles in his eye. Clay is the younger one, all straight lines and a long, blond ponytail. He leads me over to the poles, hands me one, and starts walking over to a bucket under a large, full willow. I don't think he's heard me. He starts talking about bait, but I've still got my hands out, holding everything at a distance from my body. "I know nothing about *any* of this," I say.

"OK," he says, then grabs a practice pole, short and plastic like a toy, each part a different primary color. "Bring it back over your shoulder just a little, then give a slight flick of your wrist and release the button at twelve o'clock." It makes perfect sense. I try it. No problem. I do it twice more to be sure.

We go squat by the willow and the bucket of bait. "Now for the gross part," he says, reaching into the bucket.

I've known I would have to do this, but right now in the face of it, I'm really wishing I hadn't come. "It's not the worms that're the gross part—they don't bother me," I start to say.

As I speak, I'm aware that it's not just killing the worms that bothers me and has kept me from ever even entertaining the idea of fishing. It's that you kill in order to fish. Clay is reaching his hand into the bucket of dark moist earth. I know that these kids will be told about catch and release, that most of the adults are going to be sensible about not killing things that shouldn't be caught. I also know that for many people, the whole point of fishing is not about killing. Nevertheless, there is first the matter of bait. Kill something to catch something. Worse, mutilate something in order to catch something.

At this point in the commentary on ethics running through my head, Clay has found a worm and is putting it on my hook. I look away. I really want to hand it all back to him and say "Never mind." "Poke it through twice, like this." I'm trying, but I still can't listen without looking away.

He gets a plastic cup and starts to fill it with dirt and worms. "They're night crawlers," he says, "just regular worms, nothing special. And some of these are too big, so let's see, let me get them down to size for you." And he snaps one in half.

My hands and face cringe. I feel the violence he is doing, even if the worm is still wriggling, now in two parts. "They do tend to regenerate," Clay says, not quite reassuringly enough.

I look away again. I can't bear to watch him do this. "It's not the worms," I repeat. "It's the killing."

As he continues to break a handful of these big fat night crawlers in half or thirds, he says, "I know. I don't like to fish. I'm a vegetarian and I hate this. These worms get really angry when you poke the hook into them. But it's part of my job and it's what I have to do to work outdoors."

I can't believe this. I have a vegetarian teaching me how to fish, helping me bait my hook, ripping worms apart in front of my eyes. And somehow, surprisingly, this gives me a bit of resolve. Maybe it's realizing that I'm not the only one with ambivalence out here under billowing white clouds in early June, on a lake in the hills of eastern Iowa.

It's a human-made lake, kept stocked, sitting in a valley among some pretty steep hills. There's a footpath almost all the way around, and mowed grass between path and water's edge. In some spots, there's low prairie growing up behind, and in some there are pine and spruce groves. About a half mile down from where we are at the boat ramp is a sloping sand beach, empty today except for a black Lab that swims out and back.

I pick up my plastic cup, my rod and reel, and my whimpering resolve. I head to the shore over the small footbridge, beyond a tall hedge. I walk slowly, observing. Several older folks, both men and women, have already settled themselves on a cement post or lawn chair. One man with a face like leather and a wrinkled wool plaid shirt has a small, tan dog on a rope. He smiles at me as I bend to rub the dog's underbelly. I pause to observe more. I know there is fishing etiquette but I don't know what it is. I don't know anything, except now I know to release the button at twelve o'clock and to pierce the worm twice onto the hook. I want to ask one of these people for help but most of them are so settled into stillness that I wonder if it's breaking some code of considerate behavior to engage in talk.

Figuring that I've got to work this out on my own, I wander to the other side of the hedge where I can stumble in solitude. The worm is dust covered and looks inert. I hesitate, wondering if I'm supposed to use only live worms. Am I supposed to take this one off and pierce another one? Aren't they supposed to be wriggling in the throes of anguish in order to lure a catch? I decide not to think about it, test my casting maneuver. In perfect form, I manage to land the hook, worm, and bobbin about a foot from shore. As I lift it over my shoulder again, the hooked worm spins over the rod into a tangle. Clay had warned me about this. Take it easy, untangle it, try again. It plops on the rocks again. I keep at it, working on my timing, and eventually land it a reasonable distance from shore. I stand and wait.

Bobber, I think. Not bobbin. Bobbins go on sewing machines. Even the language trips me up.

I spend about a half hour doing this, watching the bobber get pulled down a little here and there, trying to figure out how much line I'm supposed to leave lying on the water's surface. When I have to rebait the hook, I find I can do it, though each time and even still as I write this, I wince when I feel the pop of the hook entering the flesh, in, and then out the other side, then in a second time, then out the other side. But I do it. I cast, I watch, I begin to breathe more easily.

I start to realize this is what pulls many people to fish. You can stand or sit at the water's edge, stare and listen. You have something to do periodically. Something simple, something that requires little exertion, little thought. I'm not to the point yet where I can suspend thought, either about when to release the button or about what I'm killing.

A young man with three kids walks down to the edge about ten feet from me. He's speaking Spanish to the kids, the kids are speaking English to one another. I notice that the Anglo adults all have equipment of their own. The young boys, an Asian family, the Spanish-speaking family, and I are the ones using the DNR's poles.

Periodically, a kid yells, more kids yell, and others shout the news down along the shore. I see them carry whatever it is back toward the

DNR truck. One kid—larger than the rest—carries a fish by its tail. It doesn't look right, then an adult nearby calls after him, "Stick your fingers in its gills!" Another smaller boy passes, half walking and half running, holding at arm's length his pole, his line, and a large frog dangling from the end. These moments unnerve me. I am the kid in the movie *E.T.* who rescues all the frogs from the specimen jars in biology lab: "Run away! Run away!"

But there must indeed be something soothing in the act of standing at water's edge with a pole in hand, because I'm eventually able again to calm those anxieties, let go of the need to rescue all helpless creatures in the world, and bend down to poke another worm onto my hook.

I'm still landing it at my feet every two or three casts. The bobber bobs, it drifts back to shore, I reel it in, and cast again. Pretty soon, there's no more worm and I load up the hook and cast again. Then the bobber is pulled down several inches below the surface—a serious tug, by my meager experience. I wind in the line, trying to gauge if anything's there. Until this point, it had not occurred to me that I might actually catch anything. Or that catching something—which is the whole point of putting the worm on the hook, I know—might mean I have to *do* something with it. Luckily, there's nothing there but a shorter worm. I cast again and discover I'm perfectly happy feeding the fish in this way.

At one point, a man nearby in a flannel shirt and Pioneer seed cap asks whether there's something wrong with my reel, and I say again, "I don't know. I know nothing about this." He tells me the same thing: over the shoulder, flick of the wrist, release the button at twelve o'clock. I follow through and it lands at my feet. He tells me I'm releasing the button too soon. I become so self-conscious of my movements that I get everything tangled up and lose the worm in the cast. He's been speaking to me from a distance, leaving me room to ignore him or not, to practice on my own, and I appreciate that. But at this point he comes over, takes my reel and examines it, then demonstrates. A graceful, effortless, almost invisible movement and a soft plop far out from shore. I grin with a different appreciation. There is form and loveliness here, as beautiful as a dancer's bend, a gymnast's twist, the swoop of a kite.

I leave the hook wormless and try to imitate the gesture. I do it over and over, trying to let it sink beneath the surface of self-consciousness. I feel it.

"That's it," says my neighbor with a note of chuckle. "You've got it."

I think of Hemingway. I think of the nature writer Gretchen Legler. I think of Izaak Walton, his book and his legacy. Of course I resort to thinking back to books. But I also think of my nephews, discovering and developing their relationship to the world by fishing, in lakes and in the Pacific Ocean, in reservoirs and dredged ditches. I think of my brother and my father—the ways that the fish they caught and the time they spent on the water with pole in hand grounded whatever positive regard they had for each other.

Doing this thing with hook and pole and bait does not mark or establish a relationship with anyone for me. I recognize it as an act of contemplation, a skill to master, maybe a challenge. But for me, none of that eases what I can't ignore: I am unable to get past the killing, the maiming, the barbed hook. I can't watch it, can't be in its presence, can't be party to it. All of it tugs at the edges of my consciousness, interfering, sucking all the breath out of me. I am doubled up with a visceral pain, which I only vaguely understand is my body's memory of earlier trauma. Still, I don't understand how other people numb themselves to it, how the images don't haunt them, don't cause them involuntary spasms.

I have tried to understand living on the water's edge, on the river, by trying to immerse myself in a different kind of knowing. I understand only that I am squeamish. That I have dipped that squeamishness into the silken cover of moral righteousness. In the end, what I come away with is yet another glimpse of my own troubled undercurrents. My unresolved and conflicted desires. A bruised spot that does not seem to heal. And a surface I do not yet wish to plumb.

Ownership

THE BILLS OF SALE for each of the properties off Izaak Walton Road are recorded in the Johnson County Recorder's Office, a new building, redbrick inside and out. You enter a large lobby atrium, two stories high. All the offices are arranged along the perimeters of both stories. As you enter, you are faced with a massive polished and brushed steel map of the Iowa River and its tributaries through the county.

I've seen this sort of thing before, in other river towns, usually embedded in the concrete of a plaza. Johnson County's map, titled *The River* and commissioned of Shirley Wyrick in 1986, is on the wall in the lobby of the Johnson County Administration Building. It is in relief, really, bolted to the surface of brick, about an inch away. It begins at the very bottom, where brick meets floor. I'm the only one staring at the wall, trying to see what's in and on the river: barns, a water tower, trees and a dam, bridges, rapids, factory buildings, ladders, fields, the Old Capitol, a feather overlaying two tipis. Around me people with business move, down the staircase, across the lobby, some in suits who look like they know what they're doing, some in dusty denim and feed caps who also seem to know where to go, past me, around me.

The river reaches its fingers over and behind the open-work staircase that takes you up to the second floor, to the Recorder's Office, the City Assessor's Office, and the County Board of Supervisors' Office. The Auditor's Office is on the first floor. Wide, open, welcoming counters offer entrance into wide, open office spaces. There's light, there's a sense of clean efficiency. But when you go inside the offices and seek the records that are their reason for being, you find yourself thrown back upon a century-old kind of recordkeeping. Heavy, awkward, leather-bound books of deeds, their spines carrying gilded lettering: Death Records, Deeds, Birth Records. Page after page of handwritten entries, varying colors of inks and slanted script. Rows and rows of small file drawers holding five-by-seven cards with irregularly faint typed lettering, often crossed out with ruled penciled lines or carefully printed numbering. I spend days going from one office to the other, crossing the lobby as easily and mindlessly as cars now cross over the river, back and forth with one piece of information from one office—the book and page number where a deed was recorded—back to another where that book is shelved on its side, stacked on top of dozens and dozens of other books just like it, which will tell me another piece of information, a date, a name, which sends me crossing back to another office with yet a different address, to begin again on a different route, circling the mysteries of transfer and ownership.

If you want to find out about the history of the ownership of a piece of property, you encounter a maze of recordkeeping that at times fascinates, at times maddens, at times resists sense, and every once in a while surprises. If you want to know about bureaucracy, try this. It is the underside of the life of a community. It is regulated and influenced by the rules of larger entities—state and federal agencies—as well as centuries-old custom, both of law and lost practice.

Being able to sort through this depends on the care and consistency of a dizzying variety of individuals, reaching back a century and a half. I imagine time-lapse photography again, the same book, decade after decade, the clothing and office equipment changing, sometimes slightly, sometimes dramatically, but each one entering, by hand, the book and page number, the date, the required notary seal. There is always a designated someone who copies information into the Transfer Book, which smells like must, like a giant version of account books my grandmother used to give me, green-lined paper, red leather corners. Each one of them at least four times the size of my laptop computer. Entries handwritten, some complete, some not, some legible, some questionable. Some bear evidence of laziness or shorthand. When I am looking to see what happened to a particular parcel, I find in the Transfer Book only "Part of SW 1/4 SW 1/4." Which part, I am left to discover elsewhere.

To have first identified which parcel to trace, I have to search through plat maps. The Johnson County Auditor's Office maintains nice-sized ones, entirely up-to-date. When a parcel changes hands, the intern or clerk in the office locates the appropriate map, pulls it out of its protective plastic sleeve, and corrects it, in pencil. The plat maps are published periodically. But they are published, it seems, by anyone—an insurance company or grange, for example—and at random intervals. At the State Historical Society of Iowa, I find a Rural Farm Directory, which lists all those individuals farming the county and provides their addresses, and the township, section, and range of the parcel.

I also find Johnson County Atlases for a number of years, but it takes me months of comparing maps to realize that in some years the mapmaker has drawn things a bit askew. It isn't just that the course of the river has shifted, which it did at one point. These discrepancies have to do with not being able to get the bend in the river just where it should be.

In addition, you need to go to the Assessor's Office, where you can get the record of the assessed value of the property over the past number of years, which these days includes photograph, name and address of the owner, a notation about the purchase price of the property, a drawing of the footprint of any structures on the property, and a list of improvements. Because these offices are (and will be for some time to come) in the process of switching over to computerized versions of these records, complete with digital photographs, they will almost always, if you ask, give you the computer printout, and then they will pull out and photocopy the five-by-seven orange index card on which all this information was previously recorded. Because it was recorded by hand, there are words and figures crossed out or added, in pencil, in red ink, neatly or haphazardly. The history of ownership and also of recordkeeping is preserved. But not for long. What the computer records erase is the palimpsest that a piece of cardstock can contain. They erase the confusion but also the story.

On this record, the most important piece of information is the book and page number on which the deed is recorded. Those books are held by the County Recorder. A different office, a different set of large, heavy, very old books, filled with page after page of deeds of all sorts in the order in which they were brought to the Recorder's Office.

In this way, I spend weeks circling around the mystery of the property on Camino del Rio, which at various times and in different records is described as Gov Lot 5, on C. Showers land; or Showers Addition; or Southwick #7; or section 27, township 79, range 6, parcel no. 39679000; or 10-27-451-012 (which I learn means that this is lot 12 of parcel 451); or most recently, Picnic Point Subdivision building on leased land Lot 1 Site #81.

The line of ownership of the cabin on Camino del Rio, however, is brief.

In July 1977, Violet McNeal sold it to R for $2,000. The bill of sale describes it—because it is a building on leased land—only as "Cabin on Site 81, Showers Addition, Johnson County, Iowa."

According to other public records, Stephen Gorman and Violet Gorman entered into a contract to purchase the house at 817 Iowa Avenue, in town, in April 1939. In August 1948, the sale was completed, for the sum of one dollar, to Mrs. Violet McNeal, formerly Violet Gorman, who lived there until she died on August 6, 1981. There is no record that she ever lived on Camino del Rio, or as it was known before 1989, Rural Route 3.

There is no record of the cabin prior to the sale from Violet to R. In the public record, it is as if, like Brigadoon, it just appeared out of the mist.

Violet is buried in Memory Gardens Cemetery in Iowa City, alone. The man who, apparently, had been her husband at one time is buried on the other end of the same cemetery. Their respective obituaries make no mention of having been married, although the same children are listed in each as survivors.

Later, still searching through the deed and record books in the offices of the Johnson County Administration Building, I come upon what seems to be a random yet puzzling convergence. I discover that Elmar Lueth, a writer who had studied with Carl—who owned the house where I had met and discussed with R about caring for her dog and cat and cabin by the river—had, while he was writing in Iowa City and before he returned to Germany, lived in Violet's house at 817 Iowa Avenue. I don't have anything to make of this, but it is a fact I am unwilling to let go.

Violet had owned the cabin but the cabin was "on leased land." Someone else owned the land. There was the history of the cabin in which I lived, but there was also the history of the land, a history harder to trace, more complicated to understand, conflicted, of course, down to the very notion of ownership.

I walk the road, fingering all these connections like the chunk of gravel I carry in my fleece jacket, trying to imagine a life before there was a cabin or a road.

James McCollister's farm

WHEN I DRIVE FROM town south on Riverside to get to Izaak Walton Road, I am on the west side of the river. On the east side, it's Gilbert Street that parallels the river going south. Beyond the last business and office suite, just over the railroad tracks, Gilbert Street becomes Sand Road and the road rises slightly. On the other side of the hill—opposite the Napoleon Park softball fields and the new site of the Iowa City Streets Department—there's a drive on the left. By the time you see it, and turn to look up the drive, you've passed it and can only catch a glimpse of the two-story redbrick Victorian house halfway up the hill. On either side of the drive is a well-worn fence, with painted letters barely still visible: "Site of first farm in Johnson County" on one side, and "Philip Clark farm—" on the other.

▲

The first land claim in Johnson County was made by Philip Clark on section 27 of Lucas township. In 1864, James McCollister—who had come with his father from Ohio to Johnson County in 1855—bought the farm from Philip Clark for "the sum of Six thousand Dollars, in hand," according to the neatly handwritten deed on file in the Johnson County Recorder's Office. By 1913, the farm was eight hundred acres and was being called "one of the finest estates in Iowa." At least some portion of it stayed in the family until 2003, at times being farmed by tenants. Keep heading south on Sand Road, and you can see that it must have been an impressive farm. After the hill with the house, the land immediately levels out. Some of the farm is still in crops. But much of it is now being dug (and has been since 1975) by the S&G Materials Company. In other words, sand and gravel. Huge mounds of it, beside large water-filled holes.

According to *Leading Events in Johnson County, Iowa, History*, in that same year that he bought the land, James McCollister "began the erection of a new brick residence, which he added to from time to time until it has reached very large proportions, being one of the most stately mansions in Johnson County, with every modern improvement." From then until 1974, the house was never sold and never had a mortgage on it, the deed passing from James to his grandson Charlie Showers.

▲

When I looked up that driveway one day in June, there was a black pickup truck parked to the side and two or three people sitting on the porch. It was a scene strangely similar to, yet obviously updated from, the posed photo in *Leading Events in Johnson County, Iowa, History* with the family lined up in front of the porch, including someone who appears to be a farmworker joining them, and a horse and carriage to the side.

▲

Land and ownership convey character, at least according to these histories: "Stability and continuity are marked traits of James McCollister. This is proven by the fact that he has resided continuously on the farm he first purchased in Johnson County and has developed, improved, and maintained the same without mortgage indebtedness. It is further illustrated by the fact that he has uninterruptedly voted the straight democratic [sic] ticket for fifty-five years." At one point in time, James McCollister and this farm, which included the land on the other side of the river off Izaak Walton Road, were part of a grand narrative.

▲

In 1883, the *History of Johnson County, Iowa 1836–1882* listed some of the native animals to be found, according to "old hunters and early settlers." Red- and white-tailed deer, an occasional elk, but no buffalo or antelope. Catamounts, also known as mountain lions. Gophers, otters, beavers, minks, muskrats, weasels, wolves. Skunks, "sometimes called pole-cat; plenty of them." Of squirrels, black, gray timber, fox, pine, flying, striped, gray, and ground. Black bees were native, but the introduced Italian bees had by that time so interbred that "there is rarely a swarm of the pure native black bees left." Rattlesnakes, bull snakes, water snakes, garter and green and glass snakes, and bears. "Very few bears have been killed in this county; one was a stray fellow, who wandered along down the river, was chased by men and dogs, and was finally overtaken and pitchforked to death near where the county fairground is now located." There were bounties paid for the scalps of lynxes, wildcats, gophers, and wolves, both full grown and whelp. White swans, pelicans, wild geese, sandhill cranes, bittern, blue herons. Ducks and loons, killdeers and snipes, sandpipers, terns, and gulls. English sparrows. "Somebody introduced the pestiferous English sparrow at Iowa City. Whoever it was, he ought to read Secretary Shaffer's report on this bird to the State Agricultural Society, and then go out and scrape himself for a Job's fool." Frogs and toads, which live "entirely on slugs, worms and insects that are injurious to the farmer; and farm children should be taught never to kill a toad."

No mention of eagles or owls, or, as I later realize, of wild turkeys.

▲

At the State Historical Society, I scroll through the microfilms of the

1870 Atlas of Johnson County Townships. And then the 1889, the 1900, the 1913 and 1917, and the 1939 atlases. In the Atlas of Johnson County for 1900, a photograph of James McCollister appears in the section of "Prominent Farmers of Johnson County." James owned and farmed 140 acres on this side of the river and more than 200 acres on the other side, where R's cabin sits. Early on, the plat map shows it as wooded, but then not. Opening each atlas to the same page, my eyes blur—it is like a flip-book, the same line drawing changing slightly each time, seeming to move or evolve. By the 1939 atlas, US 218 is dissecting the property.

At the Johnson County Assessor's Office, I am handed the record card for the portion of James McCollister's farm on which now sits Izaak Walton Road, and the gravel road, and the cabin, all on the thumb of land inside the bend in the river. On it are three names: James McCollister, Hedwig P. Showers (the widow of his grandson), and the current owner.

Later in the afternoon with the sun not yet sinking, I look at the sweep of land on the west side of the river as I drive south along Riverside, around the curve past the airport. All of this was farmland, this road not even here. And suddenly it dawns on me: How could James alone have farmed all the land these maps show he owned? How would he have gotten to the acres on this side of the river? There were none of the several bridges or roadways now making it effortless—mindless, even—for hundreds of drivers to cross the river every day, multiple times, probably, as I have done today just going to Hancher Auditorium and then the State Historical Society, and then back down to Riverside again. One history of Johnson County says that the river "in early days had to be ferried when the water was high, and in some places could be forded when the water was low." Sturgis Ferry was built in 1840, right there across from the airport, on the west side of the river at about the place on the east side where the short-lived town of Napoleon, would-be county seat, had been.

I turn on to Oak Crest Hill Road, then Izaak Walton Road, knowing I still haven't grasped the picture yet and won't anytime soon. I ask myself, do I really want to know all these details, start to see all this differently, with the eyes of fact? Will knowing all this change it as a place that brings me to such deep comfort?

I take the left fork, bump from concrete to gravel, and enter the tunnel of trees. A lone adult bald eagle flies straight-line across the road, not even at treetop height, slow wing beats, as always without any sense of hurry, with a deliberateness that seems like communication. I keep thinking the eagles are gone. I keep looking for and not finding them. But then when I'm not looking, when I have told myself no, they really are gone, they appear, and always with them, a deep intake of wonder, as if some part of me also bows and lifts with them, taking off downriver.

First records

WHEN OWNERSHIP OF LAND in Iowa first came into being in September 1836, it was John Gilbert who was midwife. It was he who made it possible for Philip Clark and Eli Myers, the next year, to settle on the banks of the Iowa River in what came to be Iowa City.

By 1836, Gilbert was agent for the American Fur Company trading post on the Iowa River, south of where I sit now but on the east side of the river, near where Sand Road came to be. Apparently, he had good relations with the people who were already living here, trading with the three Meskwaki villages on this side of the Iowa River. In histories of eastern Iowa, Gilbert is referred to repeatedly as the first white man in the territory. Eventually, he separated himself from the American Fur Company and began trading on his own. His second trading post was sited in what came to be called Napoleon, and it was probably this building that was used as the first courthouse in Johnson County.

It turns out that John Gilbert was not his real name, that it was trouble in business, among other things, that led him—according to the first sheriff of Johnson County, who knew him—to abandon his home and settle here. It turns out that, like me, he had been a scholar, a native of New York who lived in Michigan before he came to the land along the Iowa River.

In the fall of 1836, Philip Clark traveled from Elkhart County, Indiana, in company with Eli Myers, west across the Mississippi to what was then known as the Black Hawk Purchase, looking for some place to settle. They met Gilbert, who showed them some suitable land near his trading post.

Philip Clark's was the first settlement of a land claim in Johnson County.

Clark and Myers returned to Indiana that winter, and early in the spring of 1837, they were back in time to break and plant their forty acres each.

In 1839, there was some negotiation, according to local historian Loren Horton, to make Napoleon the seat of Johnson County.

Local histories recount stories about both Clark and Gilbert that include shady business dealings, cheating, scheming, lying to government officials, and alleged complicity in an attempted lynching and an eventual death.

In the spring of 1850, Philip Clark left his farm and his wife, and with "a splendid outfit of horse teams," headed west to mine gold in California. He stayed for seven years, then returned to Iowa City "to find his wife estranged, his great farm sold and his home destroyed by the villainy of his trusted agent and friend. After a long contest with a gang of thieves and their employers," Clark got his property back but eventually had to sell it all in order to pay delinquent taxes, and left Johnson County.

I walk this land, along this river, trying to imagine before Philip Clark's and Eli Myers's plows broke the land. There would have been fabled tallgrass prairie as far as the horizons, with wooded areas of cottonwoods and willows along the river. But nowhere in the records does anyone describe or even mention the prairie. Only that the sod was broken.

First nations

ARCHAEOLOGISTS, USING RADIOCARBON DATING, know that people have lived on the banks of the Iowa River for at least twelve to thirteen thousand years. Indians know by their own oral history that they've always been here.

Here is the edge of the very large Hopewell Interaction Sphere, the name given to indicate a wide range of trade, evidenced by the elaborate artifacts and exotic trade materials found across this area, according to a report by the Office of the State Archaeologist of Iowa about the Sand Road Heritage Corridor. The artifacts include shark teeth and marine shells from the Gulf of Mexico, mica from the Appalachian mountains, obsidian from Wyoming, copper from Lake Superior. During the late prehistoric period of 1000–1700 CE, evidence tells archaeologists that peoples of the Oneota culture were living in large permanent villages along rivers, relying heavily on corn agriculture.

The people who were here before Joliet and Marquette, paddling down the Mississippi in 1673, stepped out of their boats where the Iowa joins it, belonged to at least seventeen different tribes, among them Ioway, Sauk, Meskwaki, Sioux, Potawatomi, Oto, and Missouri. Trading artifacts start showing up in excavated town sites from that time. At the time of contact, the Ioway and Oto had been here for at least two thousand years.

When metal bowls and guns began to be used by the people, they slowly stopped making clay and ceramic pottery. When flintlocks were available, many stopped using bows and arrows. With the disappearance of distinctive ways of making and decorating clay pottery, small and large differences among styles and stories disappeared. It might be described as an earlier instance of the McDonald's-ization of American culture.

At the time that Philip Clark arrived in what would become Johnson County in the state of Iowa, there were towns of Sauk and Meskwaki Indians settled here. About a thousand people lived in Chief Wapashashiek's village located between what is now Sand Road and the river. These villages and John Gilbert's trading house, as well as the town of Napoleon, were all located on the east side of the Iowa River, along with most of the original and central settlements of what would become Iowa City. Sand Road was an Indian trail.

The stories of how, by 1832, the land ended up being occupied, claimed, staked, divided, partitioned, and annexed by the United States government involve familiar parties, familiar alignments, too-familiar patterns. There were, among others, the Sauk, the Meskwaki, the Sioux, the British in Canada, the colonists, then Americans. One chief wanted to collaborate with the whites against the Sioux. One chief had spent three decades resisting the Indian removal policy of the United States government. The Meskwaki went to Washington, DC, to press their claim for the territory of Iowa. An Ioway man made a map of villages and migration routes to document that this already was their land.

By the time of the Black Hawk Purchase in 1832, by which the United States bought the lands along the Iowa River, these were the only lands that the Sauk and Meskwaki had left. Pressing at the edges was a white population of 10,531 and growing. As one historian put it, describing the final payments and agreements four years later, "For a total of $375,000 the United States thus acquired a parcel of choice land for the future use of white settlers, and brought about the almost total extinction of the Sauk and Meskwaki in this region. That these particular Indians were generally very friendly to the whites, especially under Chief Keokuk's leadership, seems to be a fact that was overlooked."

James McCollister, who in the late 1800s farmed what had been the village of Meskwaki chief Wapashashiek, reportedly plowed up many bones of buried Indians.

Sometime in the 1830s, a Meskwaki man gave to a white military officer a pictograph, in ink on paper, of over a hundred different species of animals in Iowa. Many of them are no longer here.

What is left are names. I drive streets named Keokuk, Dodge, Gilbert, and Clark. And once again I realize I am following a trail of loss.

First flood

From Devonian sea to the river outside my door

IN GEOLOGICAL TERMS, EVEN the earliest human habitation is recent—just a bit less than 2 million years ago.

Before the Meskwaki and Sauk and Hopewell, before there were prairies, before woolly mammoths and giant sloths and mastodons, before there were mammals on the earth at all, way before dinosaurs existed, before seed ferns and fungi, all of Iowa was covered by a vast sea.

In one of the buildings on the Pentacrest surrounding shiny-domed Old Capitol is Iowa Hall, which catalogs 500 million years of the state's geology, culture, and ecology. In one of its displays, you can view a column that stretches from floor to ceiling. Geologists use these stratigraphic columns to show the age of the rocks in a particular area, the age of the earth. The column is marked off in different size chunks, the twelve eras of the earth's crust. Bedrock in this part of eastern Iowa is from the Devonian period. You have to go eight periods or strata of earth and bedrock, down the column, older and longer ago than when humans first appeared, before you get to the Devonian age, dated 375–400 million years ago, give or take a few million one way or the other.

Unlike most nine-year-old boys, I cannot keep in my head or get my mouth to remember the order or even all the names in the column. I cannot remember if Precambrian is older or more recent than Devonian, when the Cambrian explosion and when the Permian great mass extinction happened, whether these were before or after the Triassic mass extinction, and whether dinosaurs came before or after. The only reason I remember Devonian is because now it is the name of a small gorge at the base of the Coralville Reservoir spillway where a campground used to be.

In the Devonian period, the continents were in a completely different configuration. Most museums of natural history will now show you a visual display that maps what is understood of the ancient movement of the continents over the recognizable, current geographic shapes, including some sort of "you are here" marker. According to current understanding of this continental movement, all of Iowa—indeed most of North America—was not only under water but also near the equator.

In Iowa Hall on the first floor, you can view a number of displays that show what Iowa was like long ago, in a sequence of dioramas of the successive periods. As in most contemporary museums, you wander in wiggly mazes of halls, not straight lines. In the diorama for the Devonian period, a huge armored fish seems to come at spectators from a murky, dark sea, about to devour a school of smaller fish. This fish is about as big as a rotund man and is named Dunkleosteus. The diorama reproduces a coral reef based on fossils found in the Iowa City area. In the coral reefs are coral, brachiopods, and trilobites. Many of these look like the pill bugs in my garden.

At some point, the sea disappeared. There is nothing in the displays or in the material I gathered later from the DNR that describes how this happened. It must have been a slow shrinking, drier climates, upheavals of the land bottom as over the millions of years more coral and brachiopods and trilobites settled to the bottom of the seafloor. Things died and piled up. Land emerged. Dunkleosteus fled or was stranded in water not deep enough for it to move. Rocks were ground down, vegetative matter decayed, sand piled up and, with more geologic changes, eventually, 300 million years later, became the dirt out of which the prairies emerged.

Everywhere there is upheaval, even in the ages before humans.

Shifting tectonic plates lift layers of bedrock; glaciers erode rock and earth; riverways slice through rock. The record is uneven, or buried, or washed away.

I've lost track of how many times I've returned to the exhibit in Iowa Hall, to its dusty old display cases, all of them trying to tell the stories of change, of flood and catastrophe, of devastation and quiet emergence.

When the waters overtopped the spillway by four and a half feet at the Coralville Reservoir for the weeks between July 5 and August 2, 1993, a roaring wall of water first hit a concrete apron, then tore on down onto the Lower Cottonwood Campground, moving at high speed. It tore away vegetation, trees, pavement, silt, sediment, and boulders, and when the water receded, it had exposed the 375-million-year-old Devonian ocean floor: an enormous horizontal surface of limestone bedrock.

It looks like a desolate expanse. Nothing worth going down into the gorge for. But in fact, the horizontal sheets of bedrock were filled with fossils: coral heads, crinoids, brachiopods, bryozoa, trilobites, and part of Dunkleosteus, the thirty-five-foot giant fish—some of most things that lived at the bottom of that shallow inland sea. Four hundred million years ago.

At first, all anyone saw was destruction. You can see some of it, and the force of the water, in a film on YouTube, made by the US Army Corps of Engineers and titled *Great Flood of 1993 at Coralville Lake*. But it turns out that, as its narrator says, there was enormous interest in what no human eyes had ever before seen. Tens of thousands of visitors came to touch prehistory. Touch, and take souvenirs.

Once it was exposed to air and elements, of course, the fossils began to wear away. Water pooled. Limestone fractured, was ground down, became soil. Vegetation took hold in crevices. Those tens of thousands of feet scuffed and wore away a good deal of the imprint. After a few years, a committee was formed. Money was raised. Interpretive signs, walkways, and railings were constructed. They built it—the Devonian Fossil Gorge—and more people came.

The river threatens, destroys, reveals.

The road I walk is covered with rock. The dump trucks carry gravel dug from pits in the earth. The river waters sometimes cover, sometimes carry downstream layers of sediment. In the marsh, plants and animals and birds and human trash stew, simmer, rot, and sink. The strata of the next million years are coming into being, pressed into a story I will never know.

Ownership, differently

WHAT, I WONDER AS I look back now, was I doing digging and searching, following threads further and further back, keeping track of all the loose ends in file folders, three-ring binders, pocket-sized spiral notebooks?

I spent hours in the spacious Iowa City Public Library, flipping through old phone books trying to trace where Violet had lived, scrolling through copies of the *Iowa City Press-Citizen* each year that the river had flooded. Back and forth past the sculpture of the river in the lobby of the Johnson County Administration Building, I tracked down plat maps, deed transfers, marriage and death records, tax assessments, tracing who had owned and sold the Showers Addition. I got one clerk to print a satellite image of the river and land for me, the size of a fifteen-by-eighteen-inch poster. I collected pamphlets from a host of government agencies and university research projects. I repeatedly drove past the McCollister house, craning my neck, then down Winter Eagle Road and Healed Land Lane. I tried to find out who had chosen those road names, which did not exist fifty years ago yet so strongly suggested someone had understood the place the way I did. And whenever I could, I found ways to get in a boat on the river.

What was I doing? Sometimes I would look up, as I methodically turned the pages of each Johnson County Atlas in the State Historical Society, and wonder. At that point, I didn't have an answer. Most of the times, I shrugged off the question, content to feel the satisfaction of doing a thorough search. But I also had a nagging worry that I was poking into people's lives, into R's life. I was pretty sure she would have protested loudly had she been aware.

I kept meticulous notes, cross-referenced them. The more I learned, the more I felt that I was getting a handle on it all, putting pieces together. Each time I connected pieces of information, I felt something settle for me, a kind of security.

Now I think that in the face of how deeply I had connected to this place off Izaak Walton Road, a connection I'd nurtured and protected over several years, I had fallen into an old habit of mind: desperate not to incur another loss, I grabbed on and held tight. I made the mistake of thinking all that knowledge would help me lay claim to the place.

Knowing had become a way of owning.

PART V

RIVER ⋏ NIGHT ⋏ PRAYER

Now when I had mastered the language of this water and had come to know every trifling feature that bordered the great river as familiarly as I knew the letters of the alphabet, I had made a valuable acquisition. But I had lost something, too.

—MARK TWAIN, *Old Times on the Mississippi*

In the middle of the river

IN THE MIDDLE OF the river, near the bend, there's a snag. I read somewhere that there are different names for the things that get stuck in a riverbed, impeding flow or traffic. I might have the wrong word. And because most of it is below the surface, like so much else here, I'm only guessing at what it is or was. Part of a dead tree. Driftwood, dead-wood, silver gray. The top of a tree branch or trunk, a V with one leg shorter than the other, pointing at a forty-five-degree angle downriver.

My eye is drawn to that snag whenever I walk out of the drive and head down the road, for the few steps where the road parallels the river unobstructed. The snag marks weather, season, the life of the river controlled elsewhere and otherwise.

One morning when I moved from the tree-enclosed circle of the cabin, light from the just-cresting sun filtering through and out onto the road, the river was covered with heavy white mist and all that was visible was the snag. Not the other side, not the shore, not the geese huddled on the shore, not the water itself or the cabins or the bend. The dark gray of the tree stood in sharp contrast to the milky fog. There had never before been a day when I couldn't see the river.

In winter, bald eagles perch on the snag. In the middle of the flow, a foot or two off the surface, it must provide a perfect launch, a place to sight and feed. Day after day, I turn from the drive onto the road, take two steps and find a perfectly framed photograph of the kind you see on wildlife calendars or heavy coffee-table books or greeting cards. Often I stop in my tracks to look. A bend in the river, cabins lining it on one side, woods on the other. The perch in the middle of the river, the eagle on it, still. I've seen photographs like this. They are lovely, crisp, clear, simple. But they do not capture it. They make the bald eagle all *too*—too cruel, too piercing, too imperial. Out on the snag in the middle of the river in the middle of winter, a bald eagle is not alone or lonely or stark. It is one point in a tableau, one part of the picture, not separable from the snag, the flow of the river, the life in the trees on the other side, the mist rising.

After a day of heavy rain following a season of drought, the river's level rises immediately. On the next clear day, I walk out to find the sandbar, where geese had huddled, where ducks had walked, where plastic bags had washed up, gone. The river is high. I scan it, trying to capture what it must have been like to live in a way and at a time when reading the river was a necessary skill. When the river's life was more closely tied to human life. When the river's rising was ominous. Although I do not yet know the mechanism or logic by which it happens, I do know that now other forces are at work here, monitoring, weighing, exercising a good deal of control over it, and that when the river rises, it is likely not to have everything to do with the weather.

I scan the river and notice a pattern in the current. I don't recognize it. I stop and wonder—then realize that the snag is now entirely beneath the surface. When the river rises, the branch disappears from view. But the snag doesn't. It parts the flow beneath, creating patterns and riffs on the surface.

River's sludge

EVERY DAY, I SIT at a desk next to the window facing the river. Days that are gray, like this one. Days when the wind is almost visible, whipping around and through the channel, over the housetop, banging doors and carrying the red-tailed hawk and vultures and gulls aloft in swirls. Days that are warm and cloudless, when the river is green blue from the sky. Every day early in the fall, whenever I look up, great blue herons are there, stalking the opposite bank, flying low downstream or up, or perched motionless across the river, half-hidden in a thicket.

One day I look up and my eye is caught by first one then another very large bird lumbering out of the sumac on the opposite sandy bank. I gape openmouthed, then realize they are wild turkeys. As the first reaches water's edge, others emerge one by one, and without a pause, take flight heading not up but right at my window and me. I involuntarily duck as they barely skim the roof. I turn quickly and see them all land and, without skipping a beat, start walking into the grass, then the short undergrowth, then back toward the woods, until finally they are gone.

I stand for a long time replaying what I've just seen.

A few times but not often enough, I have crossed the road to have a look and seen a wide V moving downstream. A muskrat, I think, or maybe a river otter. Without binoculars at my side, it's hard to tell.

One afternoon, I am standing on the river's rocky edge. I am thinking about the day's work ahead. Two herons fly by at eye's height, following the river, and as they pass, one then the next drops a glob of whitish, greenish excrement. I watch it spread and drift, organic matter returning to fertilize or feed some other part of the river.

But every day, also floating past me is crap. Right now, it's dinner plate–sized patches of bubbly white sludge or mold—something unclean and nasty. I have seen pop cans and plastic bags, tree limbs and flotillas of lumber, masses of brown leaves, as if someone has dumped a truck full, mounded gobs of brown-and-ivory foam, pieces of cloth and paper, and once what I'm sure was the decomposing body of an animal. There was one day it went on for so long I was ready to get up and walk down the road, sure I would find someone unloading a pickup or semi. And that's just the stuff I can see. I know there is more that enters the river upstream, farm runoff and probably some small industrial dumping.

When I lived in town twenty years ago, I helped some friends move on a very hot summer's day. After hours of heavy lifting and sweating, we drove to a park upstream, left the cars, and entered the river with inner tubes. I had heard often enough about chemical runoff and bacteria, but like everyone else, I assumed if we didn't drink the water and washed off well when we got out, we'd be fine. And we were. The river was low that year. As we rounded the bend heading toward campus, came out from the shadow of trees lining the park into the wide and open stretch passing the arts buildings, our feet grazed the sandy bottom—and probably lots of other things too. The water was warm, the laughter contagious.

Now I watch the same river farther downstream and wonder how wildlife can survive it.

I look up again and glance out the window. On the opposite side, on a thin strip of sand, stand two bald eagles. The juvenile is picking at the sand around its feet, eating something held in its talons. The adult is off to the side, watching, bobbing, waiting. The adult hops a few steps every so often, aiming for the food. The juvenile continues to eat. Eventually, getting nowhere, the adult moves over into the water at the shore, turns around, and after a minute, lifts into flight, toward me.

It lands in the middle of the river, on the tip of the snag. It looks into the water, turning this way and that.

After another minute, the juvenile flies over and lands on the snag too. Both weave and bob a bit, and then again, after a few minutes, the adult takes off, this time headed far downstream. The juvenile starts eating again, then spends a few seconds wiping its beak on both sides of the deadwood, hops down so that it's standing in water, rinses its face, and drinks.

And finally it, too, takes off downstream, following the adult.

I cannot know the life of these individual birds, and I do not have information about how the fluctuations of water quality on this one bend in the Iowa River actually affect the creatures now feeding here. I realize this, even as I again long to be taking flight, following them along the river's path, a road I first glimpsed when I set foot on its ice decades ago. Nevertheless, something under my breastbone, something in my breathing changes, follows, is rapt and wing borne. Something recognizes the grace of the unexpected: glimpses of a larger, richer ecology, of the wildlife that counts on, passes through and over, plays and feeds in this secluded and unwanted bend in the Iowa River. And something gives thanks.

The river's course

ON THE HAND-DRAWN AND labeled maps in the Johnson County Auditor's Office, Section 34 Township 79 Range 6 shows a ghost of the Iowa River. I recognize the river's distinctive shape and turn, where it parallels Riverside Drive, where it turns in to the oxbow, where it describes Picnic Point. It's pencil shaded. But off to the east is its pale shadow, between broken-lined edges, the oxbow flattens. It cuts straight across the current river's path right at the point where the cabin would be.

One afternoon in June, I stood over a map on the counter in the corner with an intern who was trying to figure out for me what the ghost was. It should have been clear. It should have been marked or explained or recorded somewhere.

It was about the fourth or fifth time I'd been to this office, asked for help in locating the transfer books and maps. Each time, I looked at what I was shown, certain it was all clear. I made photocopies. But after I had studied these pages at home at my table, I would find something right there in front of my face that I couldn't explain.

No one, it seemed, had noticed that the river had, at one time during the period that human beings had kept written records, changed course. No one had spoken of it to me, though plenty of people had shared stories without bidding. No one could point to any documents or records explaining it.

As I pointed and queried and persisted, one by one, men in the large open office would look up and wander over. As if we were exuding a fragrance or song, something alluring and irresistible. Perhaps it was power. Though no one ever introduced themselves to me, I had a hunch that several of the higher-ups were there. There were stories shared about how they'd "done it back then," a name everyone recognized, a reference to some old regulation. Soon the talk began to sound instructional. I thought, this is how good local government works: the bureaucracy is a maze and the paperwork is endlessly tedious, until a particular question comes before them. A question that asks them to solve a problem, to track down an answer.

But no one ever came up with an answer for me, and I left unnoticed.

I am a good map reader. Images are a necessary part of how I know a thing. I can know a person's story in abundant detail, but once I see a face, I have to hear the stories all over again, mapping them, repopulating the face with the stories. Images linger, emerge unbidden at inconvenient moments. The river's straight line, its ghost line, hangs like the shadow on the page in my mind now, and comes with this fact: at one time, the river ran through this place. At some point, its course might change again, for reasons I did not yet understand. The difference between the bends in the river now and the slight curves in the ghost image were more than could be accounted for by what is called channel migration.

As I drove back down old 218 and turned onto Izaak Walton Road, I couldn't register those changes. Looking left, then right, down the tunnel that was the marsh on each side of the road, I couldn't imagine it as a long-ago waterway, the path of one leg of the river. I could not re-vision the curves and hollows. It had run faster, stronger, deeper when it was straighter. Curving now so acutely, it ran more slowly. And it was more difficult to know. Simply, when you were on it, you could see only so much of it at any one time. Each few yards on the river, each step on the road, gave a new angle, brought new bits into view. It was, as I'd known from the beginning, a hidden and secret place.

As I contemplated the curves in the river here at its double oxbow and started mapping what I'd come to know about the various owners of the various parcels, the competing regulatory agencies that affected both river and land, I found myself wondering anew what actually demarcated this place for me. What part of "this place" was it that had so caught me, absorbed me, and taken me in? When I referred to it, what did I mean? Was it the cabin and its carefully arranged spaces? Was it just that bend in that road? Or was it the length I walked and watched, all the way up to the beginning of Izaak Walton Road? The boundaries of what I could see, of what I knew, of what I was aware— all these had been shifting the longer I stayed, the more I learned.

Damming the river

ONE EVENING LATE IN the spring, after days alternating August-like heat and humidity with thunderous rain and storms, I was watching television in the cabin when once again the broadcast was interrupted by blaring beeps, and the weather casters came on to report and track a storm. I was momentarily annoyed by the interruption. Compared to other places in the country, there are more hours of scheduled (and paying) broadcast preempted for storm trackage in the communities of what was once the midwestern prairie. It's a given, an assumed necessity. I stood and watched the changing light and rain in the western sky. Then slowly it dawned on me that if a tornado were spotted in the area, I'd have nowhere to go for safety. There was no basement, no inside wall. I got up and moved through the cabin trying to make a plan.

Eventually, the storm passed, the rain stopped, and I stepped outside to look at the dusk sky. Following Aggie out onto the road, I saw the river, swollen and rushing. The snag in its middle was nowhere to be seen. The plants and riprap that normally lined the other side, in which the herons stalked and the geese had hunkered, were not there. Had the water level risen that much in just one day? Or had it been rising steadily and I simply had not noticed? Was it going to stop rising? Would someone tell me if its rising became a danger?

I had no answers to these questions and no way to find answers that night, and so I did not sleep easily. At dawn, I could see that the river had not yet crept over the riprap, the thicket, or the gravel, was not yet at the door. And so I went again in search of information.

The Iowa River begins life north of here, west of Clear Lake. Its west branch starts near Crystal Lake, its east branch near Hayfield in Hancock County. They join at Belmond. The river, from its headstreams, is 330 miles long and has a 3,115-square-mile drainage area.

The Iowa River is the middle of five rivers feeding into the Mississippi, from northwest to southeast: the Wapsipinicon; the Cedar and Iowa, which join; the Skunk; and the Des Moines.

The US Army Corps of Engineers began its life and work in 1775 by fortifying Bunker Hill. Its engineers built the US Capitol dome, the Washington Monument, and the Lincoln Memorial. They surveyed and mapped Yellowstone. Their early work included improving rivers and harbors; they built the Panama Canal.

In the late 1800s, Iowa City asked for its help.

Coralville Reservoir (sometimes called Coralville Lake) was authorized under the federal Flood Control Act of 1938 as a means of moderating the flow on the Iowa River, and also the Mississippi. Construction of the dam was started in 1949 and completed in 1958, after a delay necessitated by the Korean conflict. The Coralville Dam regulates runoff from 3,084 square miles of land upstream, providing flood protection to 1,703 square miles of the Iowa River valley below the dam.

The Army Corps of Engineers maintains Coralville Reservoir as what it calls a "multi-use project providing primary benefits in flood control and low flow augmentation, and secondary benefits in recreation, fish and wildlife management, and forest management."

The hydraulics division of the Corps in Rock Island, Illinois, an hour east of Coralville, determines how the gates that allow water to flow past the dam down the river are set.

The engineers are in Rock Island, but the park rangers are in Coralville.

An operation schedule determines flow through the gates and therefore any changes in the lake. Gauging stations measure flow upstream and downstream, then bounce data to a satellite that feeds it to computer programs. In making these determinations, the Corps tries to balance both the needs of downstream planting and the desire for recreation in the lake (where the water level needs to be higher in the summer).

Conservationists, wildlife managers, and ecologists, along with those who prefer the wilderness value of free-flowing rivers, have taken up the movement nationally and internationally to demolish dams, especially when the dams' original use no longer makes sense or seems as important. Dams, they say, have depleted fisheries, degraded ecosystems, and altered recreational opportunities. What once mattered no longer does. Farmland has decreased; farmers' needs don't weigh as much as the revenue from recreation use. Conversation about dam removal has also been polarized between environmental activists and advocates for economic development, tree huggers and developers, nostalgia and exploitation, aesthetics and profit.

Studies measure the economic loss in navigation and one kind of recreation against the gain in spawning and migratory fish industry, fly-fishing, and other kinds of recreation.

Dam removal isn't just about fish passage; dams affect entire ecological systems downstream as well. Sediment released when dams are removed helps build up deltas, which moderate the effects of rising sea levels. The reservoir created by a dam floods and destroys land that was once the site of Native peoples' homelands and wildlife habitat; the free-flowing river where no dams exist threatens destruction of lands and homes when flooding occurs. These conversations are about control, predictability, types of use, whose use counts, and what is of value. Much of it is about whose voices count or weigh more.

Nevertheless, the success of those efforts to remove dams has been spotty—fewer removals than wished for, but more success than might have been possible not long ago. According to American Rivers, a national river conservation organization, dams have been removed in recent years from the Des Moines, the Turkey, the Wapsipinicon, and the Maquoketa Rivers, all in the vicinity of the Iowa River or Iowa City.

As far as the park rangers at the Coralville Dam know, there's been no talk of removing the Coralville Dam.

The flood of the century

ON THE WALL OVER the bathtub is an oil painting. Like the others in the cabin, it is positioned in the place and at the angle of the outside it depicts. If you took away the wall on which it hangs, you'd see what the painting shows, and in this case, what it shows is the back deck, looking toward a large dead tree, its trunk cut off at about fifteen feet. On the trunk hangs a painted ceramic moon face. Beyond it is a fenced plot, probably once planted in flowers and herbs. Sitting on the deck, her back to the painter, the canvas shows R, naked, Murray beside her. Everywhere, other than the deck, is water.

▲

In July of 1993, I came back to Iowa City to visit a friend. I had not been back for three years, in part because I was busy with work in Michigan, but in part because I was still grieving the loss of my small house on a corner lot in the Plum Grove neighborhood in town. I had not been drawn, like quite a few gawkers, by what was being called in the media, which is to say by the reporters camped out all along the Mississippi River and its tributaries, "the flood of the century." I had given only a momentary thought to whether it was a good idea, did not make a connection between getting here and the fact that I would have to cross the Mississippi to do so.

I had not yet met R. The friend that I visited lived, like most people in downtown Iowa City, on high ground, so mostly it was possible to ignore the flood. Nonetheless, I went down the hill to the university's student union to have a look and take a couple of photographs. I laugh whenever people from elsewhere talk about how flat Iowa is—people who look at Grant Wood's paintings and think of them as stylized and exaggerated. They're not. Walk around an eastern Iowa town and you know the landscape in those paintings is not the least exaggerated. Much of Iowa City is set on hills the river cuts through. Once, the sweep from gold-domed Old Capitol down to the river must have been unbroken and inspiring, even with the low CRANDIC railroad bridge paralleling the river and breaking the sight line. The hill is steep enough that walking up it winds me; I don't know anyone who can take it without slowing their pace.

From my friend's second-story gabled apartment, it did not seem as if we were in the midst of the flood of the century. But walk down to the student union and you saw the river spilling up onto the pavement, creeping into the parking lot, lapping at the roadways.

▲

In the spring of 1993, the rains kept coming. In June, 12.3 inches of rain fell on the lake above the Coralville Dam.

The top of the dam at Coralville is 743 feet high; the top of the spillway sits at 712 feet. On July 1, the lake level was 711.0 feet.

On July 5 at 10:30 a.m., water overtopped the spillway. For days, the university's *Daily Iowan* had been running a small box on the lower-left portion of its front page: "Coralville Dam Outflow," followed by a number. On Friday, July 9, the box indicated that the outflow as of 9:00 p.m. on Thursday was 16,500 cfs (cubic feet per second). The box on Tuesday, July 13, read 20,000 cfs. The headline that day, in bold font the same size as the letters in the masthead, said nothing more than "25,000?" Officials managing the lake and the dam predicted the river would crest on Friday or Saturday, "barring further rains." Volunteers and city employees bagged sand and laid barriers nonstop, but as one local business owner was quoted as saying, "I don't think anyone knows what's going to happen. It's going to do what it's going to do. You can't mess with Mother Nature."

Other stories and photos on the page all concerned the flooding throughout the Midwest. Swollen and overflowing river water had caused water to be turned off throughout Des Moines. Bottled water supplies were continuously running out. Classes at the university had to be relocated. Businesses were flooded.

The river crested on July 24. In all, there were 28 consecutive days of water flowing over the spillway. Between August 1 and 9, the gates were opened entirely. Water was five feet deep going over the spillway.

▲

FEMA's Flood Insurance Rate Map for Johnson County, Iowa, and Incorporated Areas, revised in 2002, shows all of the area within the oxbow of the Iowa River just south of Iowa City—which is to say all the land off Izaak Walton Road and Camino del Rio—to be in a flood zone.

Tom Hansen, for some years the emergency management coordinator for Johnson County, was, therefore, also the representative for FEMA. When I asked what he remembered about the area off Izaak Walton Road after the flood of 1993, this is what he told me:

> When there is flood damage, FEMA will buy out and help relocate people—if they want it. That property at Picnic Point was a mess. People were renting houses on leased land. I had to buy the houses off the property, and then buy the property. FEMA doesn't take ownership of any of the land. It finds a government agency, like a county, to take it. So the county owns the land, and it is supposed to be able to revert back to wetlands or whatever. The county has to leave it, undeveloped, forever. One of the people who lived on those parcels on Picnic Point went around organizing the rest of them, so we had a town meeting and I explained the process.

According to Hansen, settling with several of the residents was difficult. One of R's neighbors at the time "swears she got cheated by the county." Hansen explained, "I pay 1.5 times the taxable amount, plus $600 for moving, plus $1,200 for the inconvenience. She was the one yelling the loudest that her place had low valuation, but she hadn't even paid the taxes on it. And it was just an old raggedy trailer house." FEMA bought three parcels from the man who owns the land. During the period he was trying to settle, R was apparently in Belize, and by the time letters reached back and forth between them, he says, the program had ended.

After 1993, more projects were initiated to better manage the watershed areas in the communities around Iowa City.

From Kate Klaus I learned that when the rains came in 1993—when the Coralville Reservoir overflowed the spillway with such force that it scraped away the bedrock down to the Devonian layer, and the Iowa River overflowed its banks so much that university buildings were sandbagged but flooded anyway—there was no way to get to the houses off Izaak Walton Road except by boat. Inky the cat lived on the roof somehow for over two weeks while the water filled the cabin, and R was beside herself with worry. In the painting over the bathtub, in the lines of her backbone, I see a calm defiance. As if once she could reach home, no matter what surrounded it, no matter what damage, she had reached her grounding and was staying put.

As long as you choose to live here

THE FRONT PAGE OF the *Iowa City Press-Citizen* for Friday March 5, 1971, is focused on another flood produced by an overflowing Iowa River, in turn caused by unusually high flow from the Coralville Reservoir due to "recent rains and melting snow."

A photograph of the rear end of a dump truck, headed down the middle of a country road covered with water, tops the story. The caption reads, "Residents in an area south of Iowa City on the Iowa River rented a truck this week to apply rock and raise their private road, flooded by high waters." Although nothing in the photograph is familiar, I knew the road even before I read the story.

According to the story, the residents had been flooded out, some with six inches of water on their floors, some unable to drive down the road to their homes. Wells were being inspected by county officials to determine if they were contaminated.

One resident pointed out that the same thing had occurred two years before.

The journalist writes, "The dilemma faced by the residents is characterized by various conflicting views over control of flow from the reservoir." Residents questioned whether enough water was released from the reservoir before the runoff filled it, which required increased flow. When the journalist points out that the residents lived in a floodplain, he quotes the reservoir manager, who could be heard as either unsympathetic or hostile: "They'll have to put up with the water. As long as they choose to live there, they know that they have to expect this every spring."

Residents are quoted in the story, in voices that are descriptive or alarmed or accusing.

"In this day and age, I think it's not where you want to live. It's where you can get a place to live," said Mrs. Violet McNeill [*sic*], a property owner in the area.

She said she believed the flooding could be avoided because only in 1969 and this year have the residents had trouble.

"Why two out of the last three years?" she asked.

She said the situation made her think the reservoir can't be lowered far enough before runoff to prevent the problem, only because of sportsmen. Some want a certain water level at all times, and the people downstream get in trouble, she said.

However, Mrs. McNeill said that in the end it's simply a real "inconvenience," and she didn't know what could be done.

People in her part of the area, she said, are thinking about building a bridge.

I finish reading and stare off at nothing for a while, so many thoughts chasing one another. In Violet's voice on this page I hear the kind of feisty resistance I know in R's voice.

I wonder: What happened to the talk of a bridge? Did the reservoir manager's flip answer—"as long as they choose to live there"—suggest that he'd had dealings with these residents before? That he'd tried to get them to move?

What lingers is the word "choose." As if it might have nothing to do with necessity, or history, or the heart. As if a person can control what they are attached to or need.

Wetlands

START ASKING ABOUT WHO is responsible for protecting wetlands and you begin to wonder whether what you hear is actual protection of actual wetlands. Whether the concern professed by the web of bureaucracies and agencies manages, in fact, to protect.

If the land is farmland, then the Natural Resources Conservation Service, an agency that is part of the US Department of Agriculture, conducts the wetland determination—that is, determines if in fact it is real wetlands. There are other agencies I consider might be involved. The state Department of Natural Resources. The US Army Corps of Engineers. The US Department of the Interior's Fish and Wildlife Service. And in Iowa, a state Department of Agriculture and Land Stewardship.

It turns out, however, that none of these agencies that sound as if it'd be in charge actually is. It turns out that the real gatekeeper is the Johnson County Planning and Zoning Commission—at least according to the confident official at the window who spent Friday afternoon before a golf game explaining that permits to make any change in land use would have to be applied for and approved by him.

He is on contract with FEMA to act as the county's representative for enforcing the federal agency's restrictions. He is also charged by the county with enforcing a land use plan for the entire county.

He has a map, published by FEMA, of floodplains and floodways. It is not the latest version of the map. Nor is the latest version on the county's website. Every office I went to in the Johnson County Administration Building told me, "This is on the web, you know." But it turned out in every instance that what was on the web was not the latest version, or not the official version, or not complete. Real estate records only went back to 1983. The marriage and death records were available from 1990 forward, but not before. The Flood Insurance Rate Map for Johnson County, Iowa, and Incorporated Areas had been revised in August 2002, but there was a more recent one. It wasn't on the web, and he didn't have copies.

The Assessor's Office, when I asked about the parcels of land on Picnic Point that FEMA had bought out after the 1993 flood, told me they had a map of those individual dwellings on the leased land, but it was "only for our use, it's not official." And it was yet another government official—the emergency management coordinator for the county, who now has an added title that includes something about Homeland Security—who did the work of contacting, educating, assessing, computing, corresponding, and paying the buyouts.

In the end, I could find no one in any agency who knew anything specific about the marsh on Izaak Walton Road. No one who had taken a look at it, no one who could tell me what regulation or process would prevent the landowner from filling it in one placid morning.

On the river

ONE NIGHT AFTER A concert on the downtown plaza by a couple of local folk bands, friends of friends invite me for a ride on the river in their boat. They live far upstream from the Burlington Street bridge dam, farther north from the Park Road bridge, across the river from City Park and the Riverside Shakespeare Festival stage.

As we drive up to a two-story house of angles, all wood and stone, they rehearse the story of the flood of 1993. That summer, the river—even now clearly visible at the end of a long, level wooded glen behind the house—crept steadily up to and over its banks, their yard, their neighbors' yards, and the road. Their road was among the first to be evacuated, and their neighbors all went willingly. But these two wouldn't go. And so for weeks, as the river rose, crested, eddied, and finally began to recede from their lives, they came and went from car to front door in a rowboat. The deck railing they show me, to which they tied that boat, is on the second story.

We push off from the dock and travel from the residential quiet north of town toward the lights and late-evening traffic of downtown Iowa City. From the river, familiar sights yield to unfamiliar sounds. Rhythmic bumping of the cars streaming over the bridges as we duck under. Intermittent explosive laughter from walkways alongside the art museum. Distant thuds of rock and rap from dorm windows. Faint water sounds, close at hand.

The water is an asphalt road, a surface we skim like the interstate a mile or so up and behind us. Alongside the dock by the student union, mallards huddle, softly burping. Bottles of beer are passed round. I wait for insight. Nothing. The view of each shore is a little bit closer than I'm used to—that's all. What I can see is the same as when I clomp and clang over the green metal pedestrian bridge, or drive over the Park Road bridge, or tread pungent gingko blossoms along the sidewalk past the art museum. From here, the river is festive.

Years ago, on a quiet and deserted August day, I pushed off from shore right about here, with a friend who had rented a canoe. I longed for a lazy afternoon; I was drawn by the image of a body reclining in a boat, contemplating willow branches between pages of poetry. Once we had left shore, I learned we had to paddle to get far enough upstream before we'd be able to drift. And even then it would not be long enough to doze, to forget oneself, the dam coming without warning unless you knew the landmarks. Nothing about fighting the current efficiently or in tandem was enjoyable, nor even challenging, just a disagreeable mess, and within twenty minutes I was back on shore.

Once, even longer ago, when I first moved to the shores of the Iowa River, it froze solid. By New Year's, there had been enough sub-zero days that one morning from my seventh-floor window in the oddly named Mayflower Apartments, I saw a single figure taking long strides downriver on its surface. It was like a hundred-year-old postcard, as if cars and highways didn't exist. I ran downstairs, hesitated on the snow-covered bank, and with held breath stepped onto the river. I didn't go far, but I never forgot its surprising revelation. Like a road, I could follow it, go where it took me. Like a road, it provided direction. You could get somewhere on it. I had never thought of the river as taking *me* somewhere. It ran by me, providing music, scenery, barrier, but I was the still point. Step onto the river and you could actually find your way to the Gateway Arch in St. Louis, could be carried on down to the Gulf of Mexico, or turn west and cover the Northwest Territory. Stepping onto the river, I knew my fear was really the same deep pull that had drawn long-ago others off on discovery and adventure. I wondered, as I climbed back to safety, why I had never before known this about rivers.

Perhaps because I had grown up on an island in the ocean. The waters I learned to swim in were the bays on its North Shore, tamed and sheltered from the Atlantic by the Long Island Sound. On the expansive sand beaches and dunes of the exposed South Shore, I sat, I walked, I watched water and shore merge and migrate. I knew tides and salt, waves and undertow. The waters I knew you had to fight to get across. The waters I set foot in as a child were a barrier even the adults around me had crossed only once. No riparian zones here. The transitions purchased were once amphibious, the salt in my body the salt dried on my skin. But that was long ago.

Tonight on this boat, the river gives nothing. Nothing of the power of its currents sucking skin. No shelter, no music, no solace. No revelation, no depth. By the time I am turning onto Izaak Walton Road, tires kicking stones as rabbits flee back into the brush, headlight beams rounding the curve, shooting over the riverbank, I remember what I had not known before: towns tame a river, but away from town, in the dark, in its silence, a river still pulls, pulls, rounds its oxbow, drags away its shore. A river sings, and if I could get a boat on it out here off Izaak Walton Road, I'd hear it.

PART VI

THE LOCKED CABIN, THE SWOLLEN RIVER, THE RIVEN ROAD, THE OPEN HEART

Before you know kindness as the deepest thing inside,
you must know sorrow as the other deepest thing.
You must wake up with sorrow.
You must speak to it till your voice
catches the thread of all sorrows
and you see the size of the cloth.

—NAOMI SHIHAB NYE, "KINDNESS"

I wish it were different.
But the reward for being
hollowed out is that the
song then sings us.

—MARK NEPO, "THE LIFE AFTER TEARS"

We are learning a language that has no words,
Of leaves, of laughter among leaves, an earth spinning
Homeward through the broken heart of the spheres.

—CHRISTIANE JACOX KYLE, "THE SECOND LANGUAGE"

I am locked out

"WHEN CAN YOU COME?" R writes me. "You know the place—you know how to take care of it—just let me know. You can have it whenever you want."

She spends more time in Belize. I come and go from the cabin as often as I can. I arrange my work and teaching life, my commitments with friends so that I am able to leave Michigan, sometimes at a moment's notice. I have gotten very efficient at throwing the cats and dog and all their requirements into my car, with clothes and books, a down comforter, a laptop. I drive what is almost a straight line for seven hours, west on Interstate 80, and I am there, sitting in the front room facing the river, as if I've never left.

And then, something happened. Maybe I was distracted because my black cat—the one who was a perfect copy of R's Inky—developed cancer, the same cancer for which my brother was being radiated. Maybe I forgot to do something. Maybe I presumed too much. I'd had a copy of her key made, so that I wouldn't have to take the time when I arrived in town to find her friend who kept the key, and maybe I did that because I had come to feel entitled. Had I behaved as if I owned the place? Carl reminded me of what Kate had said: R was like a spooked cat. Had I somehow spooked her? But maybe it was nothing I had done, nothing to do with me at all.

I had agreed that I'd return to Michigan for the month of May so she could come back to Iowa, as she always did, for Mother's Day. And so on the last day of April, I drove away once again, leaving the cabin and the land as I had each time in the past. But when I drove up to the cabin on the evening of the first of June after the long drive, tired and hungry, my car packed to the roof, I found that my key wouldn't work.

I stood there as the setting sun was reaching the top of Ryerson's Woods across the river, trying again and again to take in the meaning of it. She had come to her cabin, and she had changed the lock.

She had locked me out.

I called her friends that evening; I wrote her the next day, with care. Her response weeks later listed grievances and intrusions that made no sense to me.

She had locked me out, and I didn't know why. Whenever I thought about it, my face flushed with shame.

The next house and the next

EACH TIME I CAME to Iowa City in the months and years that followed, I was able to find a house for rent or care, either on the river
or in town, a place to take me in. Each time—even that June evening
when I found myself locked out—it was pure serendipity that opened
a way. Somehow something always came available for me, as if a sign
or a response to prayer.

Each time, I came in my car loaded with cats and the dog, books
and papers, a tender heart and still the searing pull of loss.

The black cat with cancer, who was in the car when I drove up to
the cabin and found it locked against my key, died a couple of weeks
later. Loss piled on loss. Friends gave me a place to bury her and con-
soled me with dinner. Late that night, I walked the streets of my old
neighborhood, the one where my first house was, slowly letting the
night soften the grief. I turned a dark corner, and barred owls called
above me, from tree to tree as I walked down the street, moving with
me. Calling to one another, and then, as I joined in, to me. I followed
the calls, and twice stood under a tree with an owl in it. I couldn't see
it, but I could hear it answer me, then watched a shape fly to another
tree.

Not once in the long-past years I'd lived in that small house in
Plum Grove had I heard owls. It would have unnerved and puzzled
me if I had. But on this night, when my heart was rent beyond thinking, they were not only here but directly above me, accompanying me.
And they kept calling as, my heart comforted, I headed back to bed.

The next year in the fall, I was in another place on the river, off Izaak Walton Road. I had never really paid attention to what lay to the left just before you enter the tunnel of trees. Beyond the Termite's place, closer to the river, the gravel road continued, a spur off Camino del Rio called Ocean Boulevard with just three houses. I answered an ad and sight unseen had rented one of them from Max, who also owned a bar in town. In that place there were no mice, no wood-burning stove, no traces of any person who had lived there before. But before sunrise early one morning as I went out to walk to the marsh, I looked up at an eighty-foot oak and saw a perfectly distinct silhouette on a high branch. I stood still, tried to keep the dog at my feet. This time, it was a great horned owl that silently turned to me.

▲

While I lived in that house on Ocean Boulevard, I walked to R's cabin. I went up the drive, made my way around back, peered into windows. I could tell R had been there. I stood on a bench to get a better look inside. The calendar was turned to May, the kitchen was a mess, and the bathroom was in the midst of renovation. I resisted the impulse to pick up a piece of driftwood or a stone or shell or flowerpot. Taking something would not have been much different than peeking in the window—either way, I knew, it was a violation and intrusion. What I also knew was a driving sense that I needed this place, needed something from it, of it. Needed to be there, needed to inhabit not only the place but the habits of mind, the safety and comfort. A sense that I belonged there and that it belonged to me in some way.

I scoured the internet for a copy of the painting by Harvey Dunn. In thrift stores if I saw something that resembled what I had used or seen at R's—an old-fashioned stovetop steamer, a dinner plate in old rose patterning, a blue braided rug, a covered cast-iron pot even though I did not have a wood-burning stove—I would snatch it up.

A couple of times during those years, I came to Iowa City for brief visits, and each time I would put the dog in the car, drive down

Riverside Drive and make my way over the gravel road and around the curves until I spotted the blue of R's cabin through the trees. I'd park my car in her driveway, knowing she wasn't there, then walk the road—as if we'd awakened there, shivered in the cabin's morning chill, and had just stumbled out the door.

I did not like at all the person I had become.

Circling

I KEPT COMING BACK.

For over fifteen years, I kept returning to Iowa City, and always I would first drive to one or the other, sometimes both, of the two places that had held me, protected me, grafted themselves onto my soul. And that I had then lost. I needed to take a look, obsessively touching those bruises. To know that they still hurt. To relive the injury.

Each time I arrived in town, I headed down Riverside Drive, turned onto Oak Hill Road, then left onto Izaak Walton Road, bumping over the railroad tracks, looking left and right as I passed the marsh, watching the asphalt and then the gravel for what I might be traveling over, veered left, passed the silver maple where the barred owls fledged. Entered the tunnel of trees, past the mailboxes, then curved left and curved right, catching a glimpse again as on that very first afternoon. Had anything changed? Would her truck be there?

Sometimes I'd first take the Dodge Street exit off I-80, which slants in past the Hy-Vee, then Goosetown, then sideswipes downtown, and head to my old house in Plum Grove. Once I came at it from the back, down the alley, and pulled over for a longer look. The five-gallon shrub I had bought for fifty cents through a Kmart Blue Light Special and planted at the corner was now over seven feet tall. There was a larger deck on the back of the house, and something was missing in the yard, but I couldn't figure out what it was. For days afterward, I replayed the new images in my mind until I realized that the raspberry canes, both red and black, were all gone, now a swathe of weedless sod.

One fall when I drove by, a For Sale sign had sprouted in front of Ola's house, two doors over. I spent weeks phoning back and forth with a realtor about buying it. But once back in Michigan, worry about the possibility and practicality of long-distance ownership took over and I let it go, even though Ola's sister, when she learned I was interested, sent a message through the realtor that she wanted very much to sell it to me.

Why did I let it go? Why did I not grab at this serendipity to secure for myself what I thought would fill the hole in my heart? Was it that I wanted to be on the river, not in town? I began to wonder if I was stuck in a feedback loop. If in fact the longing and the sorrow had come to feel like home, had in themselves become comfort.

The next year, again I came into town heading straight to my house in Plum Grove. As I drove down the street, before I even reached the house, I knew something was wrong. Something had risen up looming in what had been the front yard of my next-door neighbor, between my house and Ola's. It was a two-story house, with a steep roofline, but it was sited too close to the sidewalk, seemed designed to take up as many inches of the property as possible. It overshadowed everything around it, the house I had once owned and the house I'd considered buying. It pushed up against the boundaries of each, visually muscling its way to dominance over the block. It had the effect of erasing them. Had there ever been tomatoes and raspberries and chrysanthemums there at all?

It was so unsettling that I immediately turned around and headed to Izaak Walton Road for a quick look, a quick touch, willing to fool myself, as if I really could go back and live there. It was almost dark, and as I bumped over the railroad track, came along the asphalt and looked left toward the marsh, something huge and hulking imposed itself, darkening all that was left of light in the western sky. It made me jump, startled. And panicked.

Not only had the marsh been filled in but also the quarry pond—what had been gated and labeled the Johnson County Quarry, where mallards and Canada geese had stopped over, where the white egrets and green herons had hung out, where the killdeers nested.

A few days later, I ventured down the road again, this time preparing myself for the visual assault. The sky seemed to be filled with it, a glaring white industrial warehouse, with a bright, newly laid concrete parking lot. There were no trees and no humans. Round lengths of concrete, like sewer pipes large enough that I could crawl through, were lined up in front. If you had never seen the place before, you'd have no way of knowing what had once been there.

The river reclaims the land

THE NEWSPAPERS ARE USING words like "record-setting," "epic,"
"amazing," "disastrous," "massive." "Previously unimaginable." "Some
of the worst flooding ever recorded." It is June of 2008. All of the rivers
in Iowa and all of the Upper Mississippi River have been flooding for
most of the month. It will come to be known and talked about as the
second-worst flood in Iowa history. The second hundred-year flood
in fifteen years. It will take ten years and more for communities to
recover and rebuild after it.

But I do not know that yet. I am here again for the summer, renting
a house in town. I have been watching the road for over a week now. A
few days before the river's crest, a couple of days later, a week after
that.

▲

As the river rises, but before the warnings that the river might over-
flow its banks, I drive down Riverside, turn left onto old 218 and then
again onto Izaak Walton Road, bump past all that change I had not
wanted to see in the daylight, and drive to the bend in the river. The
water is high. It has covered the snag in the middle. It has covered all
signs of the sandy bank on the other side where the turkeys had
emerged, where the eagles had bathed, where the herons and the kingfishers and the ospreys had watched. But it isn't yet near the bank on
the side where the dwellings sit.

I turn my attention to the overgrowth, to the leafy cover, to the tallest trees and the blue cabin nested in among it. There remains no better word than "nested": it sits so low to the earth, so much a growth out of the earth that it is as if built with the vegetation that clings all around it.

The driveway to the cabin is empty, the shades all drawn. As I pull in to turn the car around, I try to imagine the inside, the cats waiting there, a laptop open on the yellow table, iced tea in the refrigerator, and my damp bath towel on a hook behind the bathroom door. I can't. I cannot feel the heart line, the tug at my core. I am not, it seems, connected anymore.

▲

A few days later, I go again. I can only drive fifty yards past the bump of the railroad tracks after the turn onto Izaak Walton Road. The water has filled the marsh, is over the ditches and fields, over the road, and over the dirt apron around the white warehouse, an expanse like a lake. It has filled the cornfield on one side, the remaining grove of willow saplings and staghorn sumac on the other.

There are the redwing blackbirds calling, other birds I can't identify, but behind it all, a whooshing like tires on highway. It is the rushing of water over the asphalt, its edge now levered up a foot or so and corroded like a jagged, torn fingernail, the current like a waterfall over the road. I get out and walk down to the water's edge and see that it is moving fast. Moving from left to right, from the river's side to the fields.

A rill every once in a bit, a small sunfish, a white-blue coin caught as the rush takes it sideways out to the paper-thin edge. I reach out and flip it over, push it back into the current. It is a reflexive gesture, unthinking, and only after reaching do I realize that I am saving wildlife again. Still. Wondering again if I'm doing it any favor, as it is carried over road and on into the fields. Where will it end up as the river eventually recedes?

The electric wire that runs paralleling the road dips, a foot above water the first day I come, touching it a few days later. A kingfisher drops from the top of a pole, swoops, takes a pass at the water moving over the asphalt, arcs up and is lost in a tree on the other side. Again and again it follows an elliptical arc back and forth from one side of the road to the other, a newly created feeding table. Finally it flies off over the water, away from me, back toward the river's regular channel.

▲

A week after all the roads in town have been cleared of sewage and debris, the water still rushes over Izaak Walton Road. There is less water—you can walk a few feet farther on the road—but its force as it moves over the road is, if anything, stronger, continuing to break off asphalt. A hundred or so yards farther along, the road has buckled, broken in a V like a large bar of chocolate. The huge concrete apron surrounding the industrial warehouse hangs in the air to the side of the road; all the gravel—whatever was used to fill in the marsh, the wetlands, the beavers' dens—has been washed out from underneath, the river reasserting its claim.

But for the rush of water, it is quiet. No kingfishers, no redwing blackbirds, but plenty of chirping activity in the trees. And as I walk, a few feet ahead of me there is a repeated swift plop as something leaves the gravel along the side of the road and retreats to the watery grasses.

I cannot hurl my mind's eye over this expanse of the river's excess far enough down the road to reach even the bump from the pavement to the dirt road of Camino del Rio, or farther, to the first house, its renovation not a year old, to the landowner's house, built on the berm, to Max's place down Ocean Boulevard. All I can imagine of the blue cabin—and there is no way to get there to find out—is that the water must have completely claimed it: the Berber carpet I worked so hard to keep clean, the fireplace, the walnut buffet, the shells and the wicker couch, the rocker and the drop-leaf desk, the painting of R with her arm around Murray the dog, sitting on the deck, surrounded by the water of the hundred-year flood of 1993.

The place I had known and loved had emerged from the ruin of that 1993 flood. R had been devastated when the straight-line winds had taken out so much of the tree cover in June 1998. Afterward, she had planted those dozen or so Scotch pines in back. The next year, she had watched as Hurricane Mitch wiped out trees in the small nursery she had begun in Belize. I try to imagine what R might be feeling now, but I can't. My connection to her, in truth, had been mostly only a means to access this place.

What I feel is a desire to see the place, to touch it, to know it's still there. Which may, I slowly realize, now be only a lingering habit.

Somehow, standing there surrounded by loss, I am able to acknowledge that I am tired of hanging on. I've been picking at a scab, a thing I had created myself. It was never, after all, mine to begin with, and I'd been holding on as if the place is what had kept me rooted and grounded, as if the place itself had been the source of any joy. As if I had learned nothing. In reclaiming the land, the river had taught me, in a dramatic, visible, tangible way, to know and understand in the deepest sense a simple truth: that change is constant. That there is a life cycle for a place, for an ecosystem, and for individuals. That everything had changed, and I with it.

I thought that all the time living on the river off Izaak Walton Road had given me something I deeply needed—that being there would erase the sadness for so long lodged at my core. While I was there walking the road, I had had time and space to breathe deeply and expansively. River and road, fire and silence, snow and marsh had allowed me to unclench, unfold, and open my heart. To feel whatever sorrow and grief I'd carried, as deeply and fully as I could. Not to hide or protect myself from it.

The sob I choked down facing the eagle, the soaring intake of breath and joy I felt whenever I'd see them aloft, the notes I kept feeling in my chest hovering, moving over the river. I was able to feel things I had not felt before, not in my breathing or my skin or my heart. Things I had not known were there, tamped down, unfelt, unrecognized.

But what I now see, as I find these places so dramatically erased, is an understanding even more startling than finding the buildings muscling themselves into what I held sacred.

From the first moment I saw it, driving around the curve on that late September day, thinking I had finally found somewhere to spend my sabbatical, I had mapped my psychic, emotional, spiritual landscape onto this place. And the way I had attached my sorrow to the cabin and river and land off Izaak Walton Road—the way I carried the sorrow like precious and fragile baggage, guarded and hidden but weighing heavily on my heart—turned the place itself into a source of sorrow. A tangible substitute and a ready conduit for all the losses and wounds I had not been prepared to face and feel on my own.

One more injury, one more loss.

In circling back over and over, returning to touch the place in any way I could, trying to claim and own it, I kept taking a perverse kind of comfort in holding on to the pain, poking the bruises, picking at the scabs of that old wounded self, over and over, trying to feel again the hurt.

Solace from injury, and one more injury in itself: it was both things at once.

In circling back again and again, I finally understood that I needed to return to the lessons of paying attention: it was walking the road day after day, the sensory attention of sight and sound, the face-to-face encounters that taught me to know the birds. Silence and presence had also taught me to know my heart. Had taught me to understand that I could not erase the sorrow, could no longer bury the grief, but having come to know it, could walk forward in its presence.

After the flood

ONE FRIDAY, AFTER I haven't been to check on the progress of the river over the road for several days, I drive down to Izaak Walton Road. It's late morning, and gray. The Road Closed sign is gone, and as I bump over the railroad tracks, I see the gray roadbed ahead, with no water over it. It's not a roadbed anymore, actually, but I can't slow or stop to take it in because there's a pickup behind me.

Water has retreated to the level that the marsh once was. But it's almost impossible to see the outlines of what was. On the right side of the road, there's a swath of gravel almost as wide as the road, washed by the constant force of the river over the roadbed for those two weeks. The willow saplings are either gone or horizontal. The old cornfield is a bed of gravel. The enormous concrete apron in front of the monstrous warehouse still thrusts out into midair, the ground having been washed clean away from under it to a depth of three or four feet. The field where the killdeers once nested is sickly gray brown, a sign of how long it's been submerged, and of the contaminants in that water.

The shock is even bigger when the Izaak Walton League property comes into view as I pass the line of shrubs lining the drive. It's a field of brown mud, the ground chopped up. It looks as if the ground level is actually quite a bit higher when I sight the clubhouse—the one that had been new when I came down the road six weeks ago. The pickup turns in there and I continue on to Camino del Rio.

The first house on the road presents the same vista: unrelieved brown mud and muck. Household stuff has been stacked out in the open, back by the garage. But even more powerful evidence of what has gone on here is on my right, along the road. In the past, you'd have barely realized, because of the vegetation that grew up around it, that a wire fence ran alongside the road. But now, it is a wall of trash—wooden pallets, garbage bags, leaves, detritus, and who knows what all, all covered with the mud and muck of the river as its force carried it and left as it passed on through the fence. The fence is now plastered with it.

I continue down the road, slowly through the ruts and holes filled with water, and monitor my observations: this is water from last night's rain, not the river. I need to check the road to see that my car will make it in and back. The trees are still close, but a lot of them are down. It's a tight squeeze when I have to make way for another pickup coming out.

Outside one house is a dumpster and a camper. The Scotty camper is still across from R's place—I'm surprised, because I thought the force of the river surely would have taken it. Through the line of trees and bushes, I see there are people working on R's back deck. I keep driving—don't want to make her nervous, although of course any vehicle that's come this far down the road almost certainly belongs to a stranger.

There's a canvas beach chair sitting out front on a patch of gravel. In that one detail, I know R is back; I imagine her sitting in it with a beer, her lips tightly drawn. I can imagine it as a painting one future day, perched in a corner of the cabin. I pass the red pickup in the drive, turn around, and head back out.

When I round the bend again, a man has come out front and is watching me. Do I recognize him? The guy from whom I borrowed the lawn mower? The one who brought wood, or the one who, the last time I lived there, grew tomatoes in the back lot? I glance only enough to notice that his posture is unfriendly, and again, as before when I've driven down the road and rounded the bend, I think, "I shouldn't have come."

Past the mailboxes, a huge silver pickup comes out of the horse pasture behind me. I turn onto Ocean Boulevard, the tiny spur road on which the landowner's big house sits, raised high enough, it seems to have escaped the water. When I pull into the drive of the small house at the end—the one I rented one fall after I could no longer be in R's place—he blocks me and motions with a finger. There's a German shepherd in the back, a kid in the passenger seat. Driver's window to driver's window, we talk.

"You just sight-seeing?"

"Yeah, well, I suppose that's one way to put it," I say. "You're Loren Southwick, aren't you? I used to live here—I rented R's place for a while. And then one year I rented this place," I add, pointing to the end house. There are enormous chunks of concrete piled up by the mailbox, more junk piled up just outside the door, more river muck—the whole place looks like any one of a dozen photos of every disaster scene. "I know you used to own a lot of these places—you still do, yes? But you sold a couple? I know I called you once trying to find out if you had a place to rent."

"Yeah, I still maintain the road and all. We're getting a lot of people down here sight-seeing, and a couple of the places are empty, you know, so I'm just keepin' watch."

"Yeah . . . well, you know, I live in Michigan, I'm usually here for the summers, and it just—" and here I touch my heart—"it's just so hard. I just needed to see how things were."

"Yeah, people are here, cleaning up."

"Is R back?"

"Oh yeah, she's out there, you can go see her."

"Well, no. Mmm, no, I don't think so. She kind of, well, stopped talking to me. So I just try to leave her alone. You know."

"Oh, things kinda went south?"

"Yeah, you know . . . people need to do what they need to do," I say. I know that R hates this man, and I suspect he knows this too. As I speak with him, his face and manner to me are animated both by the assurance that he owns and protects all this and by a kind of ease with me. I know that he knows R in the way Carl and Kate knew her, as someone fiercely independent and at times difficult to interact with, for her own reasons. I would like to sit and talk with him about all the things I've learned about this property, but this is clearly not the time. I am glad for this exchange because someday I may be able to follow up with him. For now, this is all I want to say.

"Yeah. Well. I know. I don't want to say anything bad about anyone. So, yeah."

There's a lot hanging in the air, and so I say, "OK, well, have a good day. Thanks." And I drive back out of Ocean Boulevard, up Camino del Rio past the silver maple, up onto Izaak Walton Road. I don't even look at it all again, although I notice mourning doves and cardinals flitting across the road. Things are living here and will come back. The brown will be washed away eventually, and the green will reestablish itself in new patterns. I head back up Riverside Drive and when I get to town, head straight for a car wash.

The open heart

IN MEDIEVAL LEGENDS ABOUT Saint Christopher, he is awakened one night in his cabin beside a river, by a child who wishes to be carried over. And he, because it is his calling or perhaps out of love, does so, uncomplaining, although the child grows heavier as they cross. On the other side, he learns it is the Christ child he bears, bearing the weight of the world. I think of Saint Christopher wading back across the river, back to his bed, retracing his steps now with knowledge of what he had but didn't know, what he now knows but no longer holds.

▲

The flood had washed across the road, the spit of land, the marsh, and had, for all I knew, made R's cabin unlivable, reclaiming it and the land. When my father became frail and then quickly died, and as my mother too became frail but died slowly, I turned my attention to them and no longer returned to the river or the gravel road.

In the face of these new losses, though, I found myself on different ground. It was as if in washing clean the land, the flood had cleared a way, and I began to walk through my life differently.

I was able to sit with each of my parents, each in their time, as they faded, declined, wound down, died. Able to sustain my presence with them, to walk beside them without anguish and without being consumed by pain or fear. I sat beside them, listened to them, tried as best I could to be a companion to their letting go, each in their way, each so differently. Loss and sorrow no longer turned up disguised with long, flowing scarves and the harmonic lines of monastic chant. Loss and sorrow sat with me, on the other side of the bed, and no longer commanded my attention, no longer tore at my heart or my breathing.

The years of living in R's cabin on the river, of then losing yet another place of my heart, of longing for whatever had first spoken to me in that place, and then through all that, living into and learning the cadences of all my other losses—the ones I had lived and witnessed and remembered and grieved and given space to—prepared me for new losses. I emerged from that landscape and was able to walk into each of my parents' dying and the subsequent unraveling of the rest of my family. Those losses were difficult, but I was not undone by them. They led me, eventually, to live and tell a new story.

▲

I am sitting in a hospital in a small town. I come here every day and I walk the halls.

I read the day's census to learn who's newly admitted. I check in with the charge nurse and sit in on rounds to find out what's changed overnight. I walk the halls, pause, take a deep breath, and enter a room.

I pause, wrap myself in a comforter, nestle in, set down the cup of coffee, and turn a page.

A friend who has no religious or spiritual inclinations asked me a couple of months ago why I was beginning to work as a hospital and hospice chaplain. "What exactly is it," she wondered, "that a chaplain does?"

I walk the halls, enter a room: I turn a page, enter a story.

On some days, I enter a room and the ICU nurse immediately says, "Oh yes, please, sit with her," or "Yes, please, they need to talk with you."

On some days, there is a daughter or husband or neighbor waiting outside the room who sees me, sees my badge, takes my hand, and asks, "How am I going to live with this?"

Most days, I sit and listen to stories. Stories about forty-five years spent on one farm, in one house that is now bounded with Do Not Enter tape, marked uninhabitable by county agents. Stories from a woman who fell and sat on the floor for thirty-six hours before someone called the EMTs to knock down her door. The story from a woman who broke a leg running across the fields to direct the ambulance trying to find the tree where her son-in-law had hung himself and her daughter, who found him, was screaming into the fading light. Stories about a man who had lived with both physical and intellectual vigor, retold by his son and daughter who were trying hard to let him live out his life as he wanted. Stories from a woman whose failing liver periodically caused such profound confusion that she was unsafe living alone, how all she wanted was to live on her own, with her own bed and her own chair in her own house. The story that unfolded from a man who kept rejecting all efforts to find out and treat what had brought him to the hospital, beside himself with worry about his wife with dementia who was home alone, on their farm miles from anywhere, with no friends left, no children who were still speaking to them, no one else to get the crops in or split the wood that would sustain them through the winter. The story of one man's broken marriage, his anguish and need to change his life in order to mend it.

Hospitals are filled with stories, in part because when you're a patient in a hospital, almost always it's because something has interrupted the narrative line of the story you thought you were living. Some rupture. Some new, unexpected plot twist. My job in the hospital is to listen to people's stories. To listen as a person struggles to figure out how the story changes. Or to think out loud with them about how to weave the new event or new piece of information alongside the threads that have been guiding them up to that point.

When I read a collection of short stories, I need a break between each one, especially if it's a collection that brings together different writers, different voices. I need time for each voice to swirl around inside my head, time to live with it, process it, absorb it, take a break before moving on and encountering a different world. Walking in and out of rooms in a hospital every day is like that, hard to step out of one story and into another, to move from one world to another, to receive each one as unique and distinct, which is how it is for the person living it, telling it, struggling with the new plot twist.

It takes more than a deep breath before entering each room, one after another.

I walk the halls and enter rooms and listen, and some days by midafternoon, I'm full up. So dazzled and weighted and reeling from the stories that I can't manage another. Each day on the long drive home, down two-lane county and state roads lined with crops and woodlands, sandhill cranes in the fields, hens picking at the gravel in the roadside ditches, and turkey vultures circling high over roadkill, images and people from these stories rise up out of order, mixing and fading.

My brother, who is not a reader and usually glib about emotions, asks with genuine curiosity, "Why would you want to do this? It's so *sad*." A friend who is not at all glib about such things asks the same question.

Each person I encounter is a story—makes of themselves a story of their life, is constantly revising that story, especially in the face of loss. Loss of life, of relationship, of innocence and childhood, of identity and possibility, of trust. The huge disruption of loss requires us, if we are paying attention, to revise our story. To try to make a new shape, a new sense, as we come to terms.

All our stories are provisional and temporary. Sometimes we need to spend time telling stories of what might have been in order to regain our footing in the story we have, and in order to know the next step. Sometimes, we have to dissect the stories we've been telling ourselves in order to find the pieces we may have gotten wrong.

▲

In a hospice room, in early-morning hours, I sit vigil for a woman who will die that night, and whose family cannot bear to be with her. In the hospital morgue, I touch the body of a man whose daughter is far away, but who needs to know that someone will bear witness to the ending of his life, will lay eyes and hands on him one last time. I am the one that the doctors or police officers or nurses call for and then move out of the way for, relieved there's someone designated to take up the work of listening, of bearing witness to deep wells of unendurable and conflicted loss.

In the emergency room of a large hospital, I am the one who gets to hear the story, to bear it, to carry it with care and tenderness while a woman comes to terms with what it means that her son was without oxygen for too long for his body to breathe on its own. While she tries to make her way to saying yes to the ER doc, yes, she can let him go, yes, unplug the machines. Or the woman who tries to honor the story of her mother, a Bosnian immigrant, in a tongue and a faith she doesn't know. I am the one to find the imam, contact the only funeral home in town that can give her the care she doesn't know to ask for.

I am there when the girlfriend arrives, takes one look at her beloved, and screams over and over "What's wrong with him? What's wrong with him?" I am the one to say his heart stopped while she was driving here, to say he is dead, to follow her out of the room and understand her wide-eyed fear of his body. And I am the one who returns to lay hands on the man, once again a witness for someone I did not know.

I sit behind the woman who is bent over the body of her husband, sobbing and keening for over an hour. She barely knows I'm there and doesn't acknowledge me. But I am there and she is not alone.

And I stand over the woman whose pink-skinned back slowly rises and falls, in a perfect rhythm, holding vigil as machines pump blood into her organs, knowing her brain has no electrical activity. Her spirit is maybe resting within, maybe hovering, maybe dissipated—I don't know—but her long-estranged daughter has agreed to allow the organs to be given to serve new bodies, and the ICU nurse has asked me not to leave the woman alone, no matter the story her family told or how she ended up there.

I understand what the landscape of loss is like, what is required—and what is required is to be present, to bear witness. To look it squarely in the face, acknowledging the depth of grief, the shock, the panic and fear that it might be real, fear about what might come next. To catch the chaos of thought and emotion that comes in the face of the unexpected, though even when you know the loss is coming, even when the brain knows, the heart is always unprepared. To be present to what a person will not remember, to catch it and carry it and remember it. Like a midwife. Like a ferryman. To re-member it into something they can carry on into the next day, next page, next chapter.

My hands extended, I catch the pieces, try to weave them into the story that was, the story that might come next.

▲

I returned to Iowa City, to a new house, close to downtown. This time, the house is mine. Sometimes driving on Riverside Drive, I pass the intersection where I could turn and head to Izaak Walton Road, but I do not. In the first months of living in this house, I awoke one summer night to a sound I could not at first recognize. I pushed open a window facing the backyard and alley, and listened. A barred owl, close by. Pulling on a sweater, I went out the back door, stood holding my breath, and waited. It called, and I called, and only when I went back to bed did I realize it was the anniversary of the night and hour my father died. Later that summer, the neighbor cut down the hundred-year-old swamp maple in which the owl had nested, the diseased limbs too risky.

When I moved to this house, there were bats in the attic, mice in the basement cupboards, rotting deck boards, and a yard overrun with Japanese knotweed. I spent hours clearing the garden spaces, digging up everything, overwintering it, then replanting, sculpting spaces and contours, laying down new beds, new paths, scooping up new plants from other gardeners in town and new friends. The bits of broken pottery buried in the garden beds, the blue glass jars, the lanterns on the fence posts—are all mine. The bats and mice are gone, the deck is rebuilt, the walls painted and hung with woodcuts and photos. There are mornings I survey the garden, coffee mug in hand, or curl up on the couch watching the snow whiten the mounds of bridal veil, lilac bushes, and yellow chrysanthemums I've carried from that first house to every place I've lived since. There is silence, and at times there are owls. There are cats that will be buried here. There are countless pieces of myself in this place, the warp and weft of a cloth that shelters me and also sets the ground for inevitable loss. I know that someday I will have to leave this house too, and that the leaving will once again scour a hole in my heart.

When I came to live in that first house in Iowa City, I followed the directions from a classified ad out to a farm in Tipton and picked out a calico kitten, the first cat I ever lived with. I brought her home and as she picked her way around the chenille spread on my bed, I thought, "I am bringing into my life something that will break my heart." Sitting with her for three weeks as she came to her life's end was the first time I had walked with death. When she died, I was as bereft as when I left that house.

Now when loss comes, I do not fear or fight it. It's here again, I think. I make room. I light a candle, unearth a particular piece of music, a soundtrack for entering the space that grieving recognizes. I know I will remember those old losses, but now I know my way through them, a gift of grace as deep and unexpected as the close-by call of a barred owl in the night.

I put up my feet, take a deep breath, and turn the page.

Acknowledgments

Over the years that I was crafting this book, I wrote a draft of the acknowledgments at several points along the way—to help myself visualize the book into being but also to keep track of the many people who had been part of its unfolding. Over those years, quite a few of those people have died. As I sat to write this final version, I found myself saddened not to be able to hand each person a copy and remind them of their gift to me.

Many synchronicities have enabled this story.

For almost forty years, I found myself repeatedly and deeply thankful to the late Carl Klaus—for his mentorship, the model of his career, his care about detail, his ever-astute advice, his laughter, and so much more. He is deeply missed. I am grateful, too, to have known Kate Klaus, whose spirit and love of trees, color, and design live on. Had they not invited me to stay in their house and care for their garden while they drove across the continent, I'd have never met R nor come to the cabin.

It was John Harper who figured out how to offer me a position teaching in the University of Iowa's Nonfiction Writing Program, which enabled me to spend six months living on the river. Without that, this book would never have been conceived. My department chair at Michigan State University, the late Doug Noverr, listened to my stories about the birds and the river and said offhandedly that I should write a book about the cabin on the river at the end of a dirt road. He repeatedly made it possible for me to adjust my teaching schedule so that I could spend more time in Iowa City, and he endorsed me for a research grant from Michigan State.

A number of people took time to talk with me at length, providing necessary pieces of information that informed these pages. I am especially grateful to Bob Lehman and the late Charlene Lehman; Rick Dvorak and Kathy Elliott in the Johnson County administration offices; and Jodeane Cancilla, formerly of the Macbride Raptor Project (now called the Iowa Raptor Project). Leigh Ann Randak, of the Johnson County Historical Society, and Clay Johnson, of Jet Air Inc., also let me ask a ridiculous number of questions and then found answers for me.

The members of a long-lived, kind, and lively writing group were my emotional center when I spent time in Iowa City: the late Barbara Jarmuth Campbell, Nancy Adams Cogan, Karyn Hempel, Loren Horton, the late Jacquelyn Jarmuth Phillips, Joanna Shaver, and the late Carol Winter. They read many parts of the manuscript and kept asking for more.

I am especially thankful to four friends who are deeply thoughtful writers—Nancy DeJoy, Sue Futrell, Joyce Meier, and Heather Weber—for their kindness in taking time to read this manuscript and give wise, generous feedback.

And I am indebted to R, who invited me into her private, sacred space, allowed me to share it, and, for a while, made it available to me when I asked. If it comes to pass that she reads this, I hope that she will find it more tribute than invasion, and that she will forgive me for whatever she wishes I had not said or done.

Finally, my spouse, Kate Carroll de Gutes, read this book in its several iterations too many times to count, then, understanding the needs of my heart, made an enormous sacrifice to allow me to see it to its final form. I am grateful beyond words. Kate is the one who catches the pieces of my story, carries them, and remembers them, and who is the heart of the next chapter.

"Once I owned a house" appeared first in *Under the Gum Tree* (Summer 2024). "River's sludge," in an early form, won second place in an essay and photo contest sponsored by the Iowa Policy Project in 2008, and was reprinted by the IPP in its 2009 calendar.